English: Practice Papers

Multiple Choice Book 2

How to use this book to make the most of 11 plus exam preparation

It is important to remember that for 11 plus exams there is no national syllabus, no pass mark and no retake option. It is therefore vital that your child is fully primed to perform to the best of their ability so that they give themselves the best possible chance on the day.

Unlike similar publications, the **First Past The Post®** series uniquely assesses your child's performance on a question-by-question basis, helping to identify areas for improvement and providing suggestions for further targeted tests. By entering the unique Peer-Compare access code for this book on our website, your child's performance can be compared anonymously to that of others who have taken the same tests.

English: Practice Papers

This collection of four timed tests is representative of the standard English section of contemporary multi-discipline 11 plus and Common Entrance exams. Each test contains 50 questions, covering comprehension, spelling, punctuation and grammar, and is designed to be completed in 50 minutes. This time is based on classroom testing sessions held at our centre. These tests are especially representative of the Granada Learning (GL) English papers, but provide useful practice for all exam boards.

Never has it been more useful to learn from mistakes!

Students can improve by as much as 15%, not only by focused practice, but also by targeting any weak areas.

How to manage your child's practice

To get the most up-to-date information, visit our website, www.elevenplusexams.co.uk, the UK's largest online resource for 11 plus, with over 65,000 webpages and a forum administered by a select group of experienced moderators.

About the authors

The Eleven Plus Exams' **First Past The Post®** series has been created by a team of experienced tutors and authors from leading British universities.

Published by Technical One Ltd t/a Eleven Plus Exams
With special thanks to all the children who tested our material at the ElevenPlusExams centre in Harrow.
ISBN: 978-1-912364-01-5

elevenplusexams
head for success

elevenplusexams
head for success

About Us

At Eleven Plus Exams, we supply high-quality 11 plus tuition for your children. Our free website at **www.elevenplusexams.co.uk** is the largest website in the UK that specifically prepares children for the 11 plus exams. We also provide online services to schools and our **First Past The Post®** range of books has been well-received by schools, tuition centres and parents.

Eleven Plus Exams is recognised as a trusted and authoritative source. We have been quoted in numerous national newspapers, including *The Telegraph*, *The Observer*, the *Daily Mail* and *The Sunday Telegraph*, as well as on national television (BBC1 and Channel 4), and BBC radio.

Our website offers a vast amount of information and advice on the 11 plus, including a moderated online forum, books, downloadable material and online services to enhance your child's chances of success. Set up in 2004, the website grew from an initial 20 webpages to more than 65,000 today, and has been visited by millions of parents. It is moderated by experts in the field, who provide support for parents both before and after the exams.

Don't forget to visit **www.elevenplusexams.co.uk** and see why we are the market's leading one-stop shop for all your 11 plus needs. You will find:

- ✓ Comprehensive quality content and advice written by 11 plus experts
- ✓ Eleven Plus Exams online shop supplying a wide range of practice books, e-papers, software and apps
- ✓ Lots of FREE practice papers to download
- ✓ Professional tuition service
- ✓ Short revision courses
- ✓ Year-long 11 plus courses
- ✓ Mock exams tailored to reflect those of the main examining bodies

Other Titles in the First Past The Post® Series
11+ Essentials Range of Books

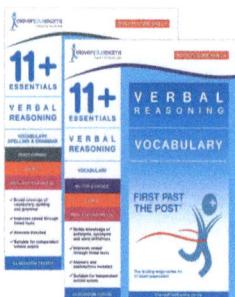

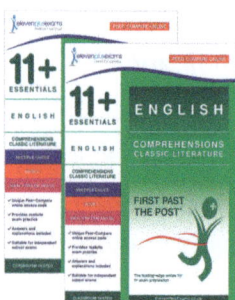

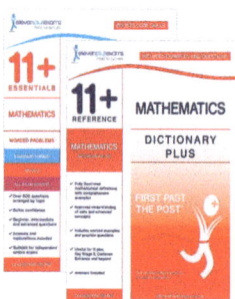

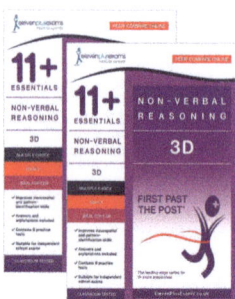

978-1-912364-60-2   Verbal Reasoning: Cloze Tests Book 1 - Mixed Format
978-1-912364-61-9   Verbal Reasoning: Cloze Tests Book 2 - Mixed Format
978-1-912364-78-7   Verbal Reasoning: Cloze Tests Book 3 - Mixed Format
978-1-912364-79-4   Verbal Reasoning: Cloze Tests Book 4 - Mixed Format
978-1-912364-62-6   Verbal Reasoning: Vocabulary Book 1 - Multiple Choice
978-1-912364-63-3   Verbal Reasoning: Vocabulary Book 2 - Multiple Choice
978-1-912364-64-0   Verbal Reasoning: Vocabulary Book 3 - Multiple Choice
978-1-912364-65-7   Verbal Reasoning: Vocabulary, Spelling and Grammar Book 1 - Multiple Choice
978-1-912364-66-4   Verbal Reasoning: Vocabulary, Spelling and Grammar Book 2 - Multiple Choice
978-1-912364-68-8   Verbal Reasoning: Vocabulary in Context Level 1
978-1-912364-69-5   Verbal Reasoning: Vocabulary in Context Level 2
978-1-912364-70-1   Verbal Reasoning: Vocabulary in Context Level 3
978-1-912364-71-8   Verbal Reasoning: Vocabulary in Context Level 4
978-1-912364-74-9   Verbal Reasoning: Vocabulary Puzzles Book 1
978-1-912364-75-6   Verbal Reasoning: Vocabulary Puzzles Book 2
978-1-912364-76-3   Verbal Reasoning: Practice Papers Book 1 - Multiple Choice

978-1-912364-02-2   English: Comprehensions Classic Literature Book 1 - Multiple Choice
978-1-912364-05-3   English: Comprehensions Contemporary Literature Book 1 - Multiple Choice
978-1-912364-08-4   English: Comprehensions Non-Fiction Book 1 - Multiple Choice
978-1-912364-14-5   English: Mini Comprehensions - Inference Book 1
978-1-912364-15-2   English: Mini Comprehensions - Inference Book 2
978-1-912364-16-9   English: Mini Comprehensions - Inference Book 3
978-1-912364-11-4   English: Mini Comprehensions - Fact-Finding Book 1
978-1-912364-12-1   English: Mini Comprehensions - Fact-Finding Book 2
978-1-912364-21-3   English: Spelling, Punctuation and Grammar Book 1
978-1-912364-00-8   English: Practice Papers Book 1 - Multiple Choice
978-1-912364-17-6   Creative Writing Examples

978-1-912364-30-5   Numerical Reasoning: Quick-Fire Book 1
978-1-912364-31-2   Numerical Reasoning: Quick-Fire Book 2
978-1-912364-32-9   Numerical Reasoning: Quick-Fire Book 1 - Multiple Choice
978-1-912364-33-6   Numerical Reasoning: Quick-Fire Book 2 - Multiple Choice
978-1-912364-34-3   Numerical Reasoning: Multi-Part Book 1
978-1-912364-35-0   Numerical Reasoning: Multi-Part Book 2
978-1-912364-36-7   Numerical Reasoning: Multi-Part Book 1 - Multiple Choice
978-1-912364-37-4   Numerical Reasoning: Multi-Part Book 2 - Multiple Choice

978-1-912364-43-5   Mathematics: Mental Arithmetic Book 1
978-1-912364-44-2   Mathematics: Mental Arithmetic Book 2
978-1-912364-45-9   Mathematics: Worded Problems Book 1
978-1-912364-46-6   Mathematics: Worded Problems Book 2
978-1-912364-52-7   Mathematics: Worded Problems Book 3
978-1-912364-47-3   Mathematics: Dictionary Plus
978-1-912364-50-3   Mathematics: Crossword Puzzles Book 1
978-1-912364-51-0   Mathematics: Crossword Puzzles Book 2
978-1-912364-48-0   Mathematics: Practice Papers Book 1 - Multiple Choice

978-1-912364-87-9   Non-Verbal Reasoning: 2D Book 1 - Multiple Choice
978-1-912364-88-6   Non-Verbal Reasoning: 2D Book 2 - Multiple Choice
978-1-912364-85-5   Non-Verbal Reasoning: 3D Book 1 - Multiple Choice
978-1-912364-86-2   Non-Verbal Reasoning: 3D Book 2 - Multiple Choice
978-1-912364-83-1   Non-Verbal Reasoning: Practice Papers Book 1 - Multiple Choice

Contents

This book comprises four tests, each with 50 questions and designed to be completed in 50 minutes. This book also contains the respective answer sheets and answers and explanations for each test.

BLANK PAGE

FIRST PAST THE POST®

English

Multiple-Choice

Test A

Read the following instructions carefully:

1) Do not open this test paper until you are told to do so.

2) Please fill in your details accurately at the top of the answer sheet.

3) Only mark your answer using a **pencil** by drawing a **firm horizontal line** next to your chosen answer on the answer sheet.

4) If you want to change your answer, first rub out your old answer completely and then mark your new answer clearly.

5) Work as efficiently and carefully as you can to ensure you finish within time.

6) If you are unsure of the answer, choose the option you think is the best.

7) When you have finished a page, go straight onto the next page.

8) When you reach the end, go back and check all your answers.

9) This test contains comprehension, spelling, punctuation and grammar questions.

10) There are **50 questions** and you have **50 minutes** in which to complete this paper.

Good luck!

Read this passage carefully, then answer the questions that follow.

Villain?

The title of 'Evil Stepmother' was never one that Ana Tremaine had ever desired to claim. Nor would she ever condescend to listen to any such person wishing to impress this epithet upon her. In fact, she rather saw
5 herself as the tragic heroine of the fairy tale scripted for her by her parents the moment she was laid in the obtrusive, ornate and ostentatious cradle, one inch smaller than that of her elder twin sister – Clara.

Born one minute before her, Clara was always that
10 one inch ahead. Clara walked one second before her, learned to read one month before her, and she could always recite one more page of 'The Rules of Courtly Behaviour for Young Ladies'. Clara learned to sing that one gorgeous tone higher, she could dance more gracefully,
15 flirt more subtly and make her dresses look one monumental touch prettier. Clara would always come first in their parents' eyes, their trophy winning horse, while she, Ana, was left to eat up the scraps left behind Clara's stunning gallop. It was Clara who was destined to raise
20 their family's fortunes ever higher by marrying into nobility, and Ana who was to be Clara's background support by increasing the Tremaine family's steadily growing, reputable wealth by marrying the richest local grocer. She a grocer's wife, slaving away, while Clara lazed
25 away in her life of luxury.

Well, Ana, as might be expected, would not let that stand. She learnt to plot and to scheme. Cautiously growing in skill, calculating intelligence and maliciousness, Ana manoeuvred as elegantly as a swan on water upwards
30 through the ranks of her small town's society, until she found a gentleman of suitable wealth and esteem to match her hand-crafted reputation.

Perhaps this is where Ana Tremaine's problems would have ended. Married to a simple but kind and
35 wealthy man, with enough rank to release Ana from the clutches of jealousy and the greedy, grasping hands of her parents. Or, more importantly, a man with whom she had two precious daughters, Drizella and Anastasia. Love is, as so often told through fairy tales, the most powerful magic
40 that exists in the world, and the immense, all-consuming love Ana felt for her two most beloved jewels was potent enough to instil life into her rusty and worn out heart.

Her daughters could not claim to have the classic, gentle beauty that so characterised the daughters of the
45 Tremaine line and Clara's own children. But Ana grew to cherish Anastasia's dimples as her heart would fill with joy when she saw her bright and wild smile, and Ana adored Drizella's numerous freckles which appeared upon her rosy cheeks after playing happily with her sister under the
50 proud and glorious sun. Most of all, Ana, with her diligent and dedicated determination and insightful manipulations, ensured that both her daughters were treated, unfailingly, as equals in everything they undertook and in everything they received.

55 It was the year in which Drizella and Anastasia turned seven years old that Ana's life took its final turn downhill. It started, as is usual with most fairy tales, with the death of a parent. Ana's husband died in his sleep in the same manner in which he had lived his life: simply,
60 peacefully and happily thinking of the family he loved, but with no conscious thought as to how his passing might affect his wife. Not that he should have been overly concerned for his wife's grief at that particular point in time, as Ana was more preoccupied with worry over how
65 his death would trouble her daughters' futures.

Ana knew that, for her daughters to live comfortably in a position, their station in life demanded they needed a father to protect them. So, Ana's hunt began. She planned her pursuit with meticulous reasoning.
70 Ana needed a husband who was wealthy and of high enough rank, who, at the same time, would delight in gaining two daughters to care for. A difficult task maybe for any other lady, but Ana quickly had several suitors. Ana thought them all quite splendid to fit in with her designs,
75 but one stood out from the crowd. Oddly enough, it was not because he was spectacularly wealthy (he was of a more modest income) or that he was of noble birth (being merely a gentleman who made his money from trade), it was the way he treated her daughters.

80 Sir Travers always brought the freshest and most colourful flowers to present to her daughters, wild from the fields, no matter the state of the weather. He would answer all their curious questions and spin tales of marvellous and exciting adventures from his travels
85 abroad. He willingly and delightedly spent time with them,

Villain?

even when Ana was not present to watch. Sir Travers acted like they were his own daughters and often enthusiastically described how happy he would be for them to become sisters of his own daughter. Slowly,

90 something began to happen, something Ana did not plan for. He bewitched them, and Ana fell profoundly and deeply in love. She had been caught in the web of a much sneakier and venomous predator than she had bargained for.

95   At the end of a four-month courtship, the couple were blissfully married, and Ana and her daughters were quickly bundled up into a fine four-horse-drawn carriage to be driven to their new home. The house -- more of a manor -- was marvellous at first sight. The house could

100 be seen from a fair distance away, and, as a person came closer, one could see a gleaming and charming house with the light of the sun bouncing off the windows. It was perfect. Ana barely managed to restrain a twitch on the sides of her lips as she stepped off the carriage to be

105 presented to Sir Travers' daughter. She was a tiny, winsome girl with ash-blonde hair, rosy cheeks, bright blue eyes and a small smile, which turned to an ecstatic giggle when her father swooped down to hug her. Ana had barely time to say her own name, let alone her

110 daughters' names, before Sir Travers swept his daughter away with an air of complete joy, leaving Ana, Drizella and Anastasia in the now gloomy, cold air. It was in that moment that Ana realised she had been duped. It left a bitter, sour taste.

115   As the months then passed, and Ana was forced to watch Drizella's freckles evaporate and the sight of Anastasia's dimples lessen, she felt the return of some old friends. Whilst her new husband paraded his dearest treasure gloatingly in front of her, gifting *his* daughter

120 the most heartfelt gifts of hand-picked flowers and favourite desserts, at the same time buying *her* daughters only identical new dolls, Ana felt her jealousy and hatred grow again from the seed planted long ago. She had never felt such despair watching her own

125 daughters suffering the cruelty her parents had inflicted upon her. She returned to hatching and brewing her schemes. Love, after all, is the most formidable magic there is; love has power to both create and destroy, and, one day soon, Ana would tear his daughter down from

130 the pedestal he had placed her on and have her sweeping up the cinders of his destruction.

   The years passed, and, for a brief period of time, Ana saw her plans come to fruition. But it was not to last. Deep in the dark and damp cell in which she was

135 cast for her actions, Ana Tremaine would still never answer to the moniker of the 'Evil Stepmother'. However, she would always, always claim the name of 'Mother'.

Please answer these questions. Look at the passage again if you need to.
You should choose the **best** answer put a line through its adjacent box.

1 Which fairy tale is Ana Tremaine from?

A Snow White
B Little Red Riding Hood
C Cinderella
D Hansel and Gretel
E Rapunzel

2 What does the repetition of the word 'one' emphasise in the second paragraph?

A that Ana is one inch smaller than Clara
B that Ana's cradle is one inch smaller than Clara's
C how Clara always came first in their parents' eyes
D how special Clara is to Ana
E how Ana always came first in their parents' eyes

3 Choose the true statement. Clara...

A always read a book one month before Ana
B flirted more boldly than Ana
C danced more elegantly than Ana
D created dresses that were much prettier than Ana's
E walked one inch ahead of Ana

4 What was Ana's purpose considered to be by her parents? (lines 23-24

A to become a grocer's wife
B to become a nobleman's wife
C to help Clara by being her servant
D to help her parents
E to eat the food scraps Clara leaves behind her

5 Which group of words best describe Ana's personality in the second and third paragraphs?

A canny, hostile and determined
B mathematical, shy and elegant
C greedy, intelligent and nervous
D steady, generous and clever
E shallow, cowardly and jealous

PLEASE GO ON TO THE NEXT PAGE

6 What quality did Ana's husband possess that allowed Ana to be released from 'the greedy, grasping hands of her parents' (lines 34-37)?

A Ana's husband was kind.
B Ana's husband was wealthy.
C Ana's husband had a high social rank.
D A & B
E B & C

7 What does the word 'jewels' refer to in the following line?
'all-consuming love Ana felt for her two most beloved jewels' (lines 40-41)

A Ana's dowry
B jewellery Ana's new husband gave her
C Ana's two daughters
D two diamonds that Ana had been gifted
E Ana's new husband

8 What did Ana value most in her new life?

A her husband's wealth
B Her daughters are regarded in the same manner.
C Her two daughters get along well.
D Anastasia's dimples and Drizella's freckles
E Her daughters had the Tremaine beauty.

9 What is the purpose of the brackets used when describing Sir Travers?

A to inform the reader about Sir Travers' place in society
B to inform the reader of Sir Travers' habits
C to inform the reader as to what Ana dislikes about Sir Travers
D to give the reader more information on what Ana likes about Sir Travers
E to emphasise the important qualities Sir Travers has

10 Choose the false statement. Ana liked Sir Travers because...

A he would answer Drizella and Anastasia's inquisitive questions.
B he would tell her daughters stories of his travels abroad.
C he brought her daughters natural flowers from the pastures.
D he pretended to be happy when he spent time with Ana's daughters.
E he treated her daughters like they were his own children.

PLEASE GO ON TO THE NEXT PAGE

11 'Sir Travers swept his daughter away with an air of complete joy, leaving Ana, Drizella and Anastasia in the now gloomy, cold air' (lines 110-113)
Which option best describes how Ana is feeing?

A despairing and relaxed
B despondent and indifferent
C delighted and distressed
D offended and anguished
E apathetic and mortified

12 Who are the 'old friends' (lines 115-123) whom Ana felt the return of?

A Drizella's freckles and Anastasia's dimples
B hand picked flowers and favourite desserts
C her two daughters
D jealousy and hatred
E hatching and brewing

13 What caused Ana to feel spiteful towards Sir Travers' daughter?

A Sir Travers bought Ana's daughters identical dolls.
B Sir Travers paraded his daughters around the house.
C Sir Travers bought his daughter the gifts he used to buy Ana's daughters.
D Sir Travers placed his daughter on a stool.
E Sir Travers valued his daughter above Ana's.

14 What is emphasised by the repetition in the following line?
'she would always, always claim the name of 'Mother.' (lines 135-136)

A that Ana is the 'Evil Stepmother' and deserves to be in a cell
B that Ana is a mother
C that what drove Ana's actions was love for her daughters
D that Ana has two daughters who still need her
E that Ana will never answer to the title of the 'Evil Stepmother'

15 'wishing to impress this epithet upon her' (lines 3-4)
What is the meaning of this phrase?

A demanding her to take a characterisation
B desiring to mark her with this title
C requiring her to identify herself by this name
D detesting the name that has been chosen for her
E yearning to gain her respect with the title

PLEASE GO ON TO THE NEXT PAGE

16 'she was laid in the obtrusive, ornate and ostentatious cradle' (lines 6-7)
Which literary device is used in this phrase?

A simile
B metaphor
C alliteration
D euphemism
E personification

17 'their trophy winning horse' (line 17)
Which literary device is used in this phrase?

A simile
B metaphor
C personification
D alliteration
E hyperbole

18 Which option is the best synonym for the word 'esteem' (line 31)?

A respect
B contempt
C scorn
D indifference
E modesty

19 'her hand-crafted reputation' (lines 32)
What is the word class of the underlined word?

A noun
B verb
C adjective
D adverb
E preposition

20 Which option is the best antonym for the word 'potent' (line 41)?

A inadequate
B dominant
C compelling
D indestructible
E irresistible

21 Which option is the best synonym for the word 'meticulous' (line 69)?

A effortless
B diligent
C hasty
D immense
E malicious

22 Which word class do the following words belong to?

condescend (line 3)   scheme (line 27)   manoeuvred (line 29)

instil (line 42)   bewitched (line 91)

A common nouns
B verbs
C adjectives
D adverbs
E abstract nouns

23 What is meant by 'winsome girl' (line 106)?

A a manipulative girl
B a talkative girl
C an endearing girl
D a victorious girl
E a repulsive girl

24 How many of the following words are adverbs?

impress (line 4)   tragic (line 5)   always (line 9)   subtly (line 15)   cherish (line 46)

A one
B two
C three
D four
E five

25 Why does the title have a question mark?

A It is questioning whether the title 'Villain' is a good title.
B It is questioning whether the story is evil.
C It is asking the reader to come up with their own title for the story.
D It is questioning whether Ana Tremaine is actually a villain.
E It is asking the reader if they like the villain or not.

PLEASE GO ON TO THE NEXT PAGE

In the sentences there are some **spelling** mistakes. On each numbered line there is either **one** mistake or **no** mistake. Find the group of words with the mistake in it and mark its letter on your answer sheet. **If there is no mistake, mark N.**

Monsters & Heroes

26 They stretched out there long, sharp claws to grab the delicious food before them.
A | B | C | D | N

27 For the warrior to defeat the foul monster, he would have to tell a convincing lye.
A | B | C | D | N

28 The shining sword was swung with precision to pierce the beast's venomous hide.
A | B | C | D | N

29 The buisness of demon slaying was a very difficult and incredibly dangerous job.
A | B | C | D | N

30 Patience, the damsel, waved her hankerchief in the air to honour the brave knight.
A | B | C | D | N

31 Brian carefuly and lightly tiptoed towards the gigantic figure to unveil the treasure.
A | B | C | D | N

32 The goverment was determined to nominate the best, boldest and bravest heroes.
A | B | C | D | N

33 When decideing how to slay the dragon, he chose the deadliest and brightest sword.
A | B | C | D | N

PLEASE GO ON TO THE NEXT PAGE

In this passage there are some **punctuation and capitalisation** mistakes. On each numbered line there is either **one** mistake or **no** mistake. Find the group of words with the mistake in it and mark its letter on your answer sheet.

The Brothers Grimm

34 folklore is the traditional beliefs, customs and stories of a community passed
A   B   C   D   N

35 down through the generations by word of mouth. Brother's Jacob and Wilhelm
A   B   C   D   N

36 Grimm were german folklorists who travelled all around Germany collecting folk
A   B   C   D   N

37 music and literature; the brothers were interested in how national identity could
A   B   C   D   N

38 be found in popular culture and with the common people they are best known for
A   B   C   D   N

39 their compilation of these tales into a book called *Grimms Fairy Tales* which
A   B   C   D   N

40 preserved many important oral stories. Many of these folk tales are now
A   B   C   D   N

41 popularised throughout the world such as: Cinderella, Snow White, and Rapunzel.
A   B   C   D   N

PLEASE GO ON TO THE NEXT PAGE

In this passage you have to choose the **best** word, or **group of words**, to complete each numbered line so that it makes sense and is written in correct English. Choose the **best** answer and mark its letter on your answer sheet.

A Good Fairy Point of View

Belinda, a very dedicated, delightful and determined fairy godmother, looked

42

front	under	onto	upon	on
A	B	C	D	E

the poor, struggling and

43

helpful	helpless	help	helping	helpfulness
A	B	C	D	E

Cinderella who was trying to finish hundreds of chores for the mistresses

44

who	was	whom	which	where
A	B	C	D	E

she served—the cruel Lady Tremaine and her two vicious daughters.

45

Although	Because	And	Despite	Even
A	B	C	D	E

they treated Cinderella so callously, Cinderella still treated everyone with

46

kind.	kindly.	kindness.	kinder.	kindest.
A	B	C	D	E

It was Cinderella's benignity against

47

there	there'll	they are	they're	their
A	B	C	D	E

maltreatment that had prompted Belinda to award Cinderella one wish.

48

When	Where	During	Around	Meanwhile
A	B	C	D	E

the time came for Cinderella's wish to

49

grasp	take	took	taken	taking
A	B	C	D	E

place, Belinda was adamant that Cinderella would have the happiest moment of her

50

lives.	lifes.	life.	live.	lie.
A	B	C	D	E

END OF TEST

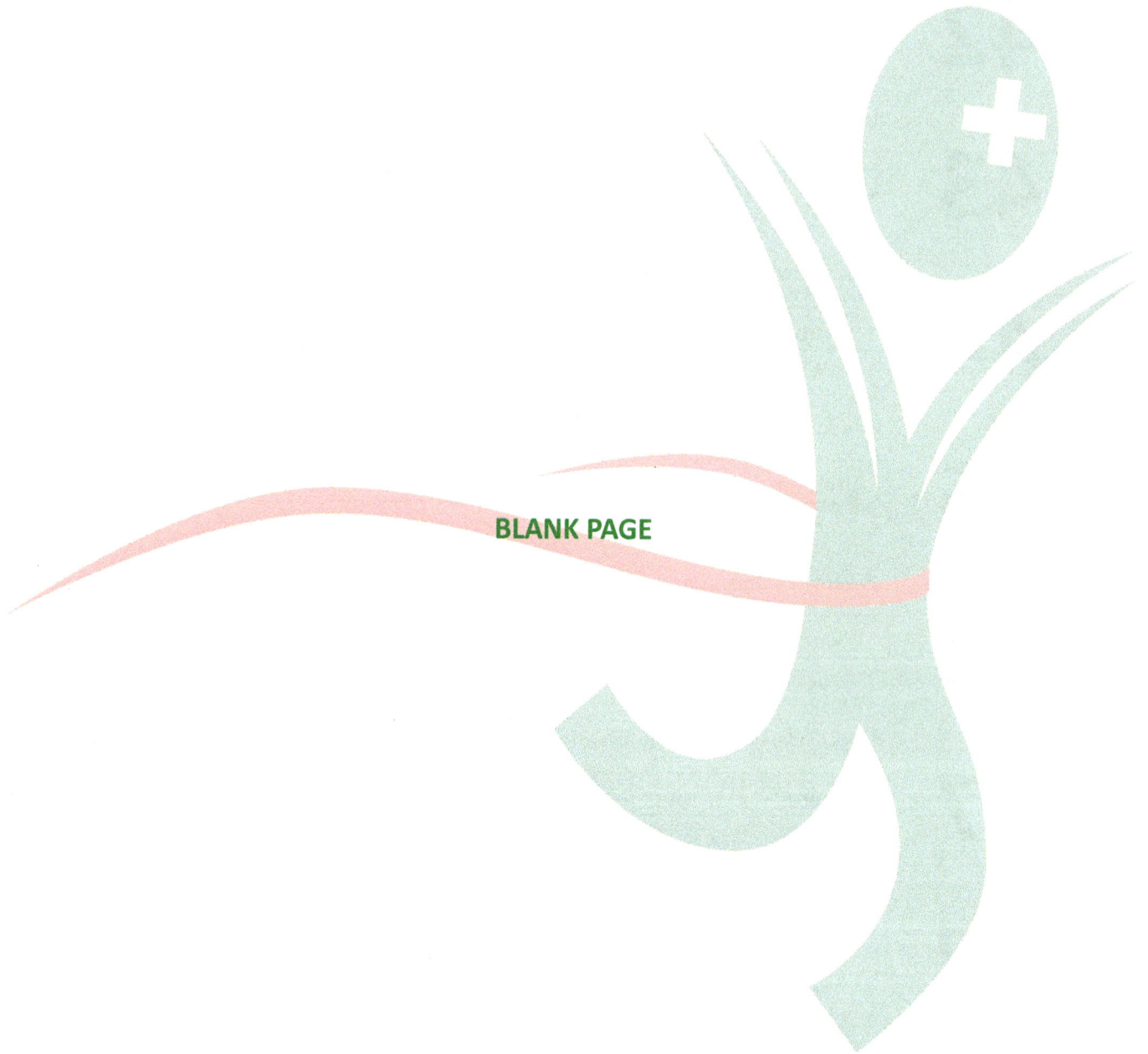

BLANK PAGE

FIRST PAST THE POST®

English

Multiple-Choice

Test B

Read the following instructions carefully:

1) Do not open this test paper until you are told to do so.

2) Please fill in your details accurately at the top of the answer sheet.

3) Only mark your answer using a **pencil** by drawing a **firm horizontal line** next to your chosen answer on the answer sheet.

4) If you want to change your answer, first rub out your old answer completely and then mark your new answer clearly.

5) Work as efficiently and carefully as you can to ensure you finish within time.

6) If you are unsure of the answer, choose the option you think is the best.

7) When you have finished a page, go straight onto the next page.

8) When you reach the end, go back and check all your answers.

9) This test contains comprehension, spelling, punctuation and grammar questions.

10) There are **50 questions** and you have **50 minutes** in which to complete this paper.

Good luck!

elevenplusexams
head for success

Read this passage carefully, then answer the questions that follow.

Extract from
Little Women
by Louisa May Alcott

The storm cleared up below, for Mrs. March came home, and, having heard the story, soon brought Amy to a sense of the wrong she had done her sister. Jo's book was the pride of her heart, and was regarded by her family as a
5 literary sprout of great promise. It was only half a dozen little fairy tales, but Jo had worked over them patiently, putting her whole heart into her work, hoping to make something good enough to print. She had just copied them with great care, and had destroyed the old manuscript, so
10 that Amy's bonfire had consumed the loving work of several years. It seemed a small loss to others, but to Jo it was a dreadful calamity, and she felt that it never could be made up to her. Beth mourned as for a departed kitten, and Meg refused to defend her pet. Mrs. March looked
15 grave and grieved, and Amy felt that no one would love her till she had asked pardon for the act which she now regretted more than any of them.

When the tea bell rang, Jo appeared, looking so grim and unapproachable that it took all Amy's courage to
20 say meekly...

"Please forgive me, Jo. I'm very, very sorry."

"I never shall forgive you," was Jo's stern answer, and from that moment she ignored Amy entirely.

No one spoke of the great trouble, not even Mrs.
25 March, for all had learned by experience that when Jo was in that mood words were wasted, and the wisest course was to wait till some little accident, or her own generous nature, softened Jo's resentment and healed the breach. It was not a happy evening, for though they sewed as usual,
30 while their mother read aloud from Bremer, Scott, or Edgeworth, something was wanting, and the sweet home peace was disturbed. They felt this most when singing time came, for Beth could only play, Jo stood dumb as a stone, and Amy broke down, so Meg and Mother sang
35 alone. But in spite of their efforts to be as cheery as larks, the flutelike voices did not seem to chord as well as usual, and all felt out of tune.

As Jo received her good-night kiss, Mrs. March whispered gently, "My dear, don't let the sun go down
40 upon your anger. Forgive each other, help each other, and begin again tomorrow."

Jo wanted to lay her head down on that motherly bosom, and cry her grief and anger all away, but tears were an unmanly weakness, and she felt so deeply injured that
45 she really couldn't quite forgive yet. So she winked hard, shook her head, and said gruffly because Amy was listening, "It was an abominable thing, and she doesn't deserve to be forgiven."

With that she marched off to bed, and there was no
50 merry or confidential gossip that night.

Amy was much offended that her overtures of peace had been repulsed, and began to wish she had not humbled herself, to feel more injured than ever, and to plume herself on her superior virtue in a way which was
55 particularly exasperating. Jo still looked like a thunder cloud, and nothing went well all day. It was bitter cold in the morning, she dropped her precious turnover in the gutter, Aunt March had an attack of the fidgets, Meg was sensitive, Beth would look grieved and wistful when she
60 got home, and Amy kept making remarks about people who were always talking about being good and yet wouldn't even try when other people set them a virtuous example.

"Everybody is so hateful, I'll ask Laurie to go
65 skating. He is always kind and jolly, and will put me to rights, I know," said Jo to herself, and off she went.

Amy heard the clash of skates, and looked out with an impatient exclamation. "There! She promised I should go next time, for this is the last ice we shall have. But it's no
70 use to ask such a crosspatch to take me."

"Don't say that. You were very naughty, and it is hard to forgive the loss of her precious little book, but I think she might do it now, and I guess she will, if you try her at the right minute," said Meg. "Go after them. Don't
75 say anything till Jo has got good-natured with Laurie, than take a quiet minute and just kiss her, or do some kind thing, and I'm sure she'll be friends again with all her heart."

Little Women

"I'll try," said Amy, for the advice suited her, and
80 after a flurry to get ready, she ran after the friends, who
were just disappearing over the hill.

It was not far to the river, but both were ready
before Amy reached them. Jo saw her coming, and
turned her back. Laurie did not see, for he was carefully
85 skating along the shore, sounding the ice, for a warm
spell had preceded the cold snap.

"I'll go on to the first bend, and see if it's all right
before we begin to race," Amy heard him say, as he shot
away, looking like a young Russian in his fur-trimmed
90 coat and cap.

Jo heard Amy panting after her run, stamping her
feet and blowing on her fingers as she tried to put her
skates on, but Jo never turned and went slowly
zigzagging down the river, taking a bitter, unhappy sort
95 of satisfaction in her sister's troubles. She had cherished
her anger till it grew strong and took possession of her,
as evil thoughts and feelings always do unless cast out at
once. As Laurie turned the bend, he shouted back…

"Keep near the shore. It isn't safe in the middle."
100 Jo heard, but Amy was struggling to her feet and did not
catch a word. Jo glanced over her shoulder, and the little
demon she was harboring said in her ear…

"No matter whether she heard or not, let her
take care of herself."

105 Laurie had vanished round the bend, Jo was just
at the turn, and Amy, far behind, striking out toward the
the smoother ice in the middle of the river. For a minute
Jo stood still with a strange feeling in her heart, then she
resolved to go on, but something held and turned her
110 round, just in time to see Amy throw up her hands and
go down, with a sudden crash of rotten ice, the splash of
water, and a cry that made Jo's heart stand still with
fear. She tried to call Laurie, but her voice was gone. She
tried to rush forward, but her feet seemed to have no
115 strength in them, and for a second, she could only stand
motionless, staring with a terror-stricken face at the little
blue hood above the black water. Something rushed
swiftly by her, and Laurie's voice cried out…

"Bring a rail. Quick, quick!"

120 How she did it, she never knew, but for the next
few minutes she worked as if possessed, blindly obeying
Laurie, who was quite self-possessed, and lying flat, held

Amy up by his arm and hockey stick till Jo dragged a rail from
125 the fence, and together they got the child out, more
frightened than hurt.

"Now then, we must walk her home as fast as we
can. Pile our things on her, while I get off these confounded
skates," cried Laurie, wrapping his coat round Amy, and
130 tugging away at the straps which never seemed so intricate
before.

Shivering, dripping, and crying, they got Amy home,
and after an exciting time of it, she fell asleep, rolled in
blankets before a hot fire. During the bustle Jo had scarcely
135 spoken but flown about, looking pale and wild, with her
things half off, her dress torn, and her hands cut and bruised
by ice and rails and refractory buckles. When Amy was
comfortably asleep, the house quiet, and Mrs. March sitting
by the bed, she called Jo to her and began to bind up the hurt
140 hands.

"Are you sure she is safe?" whispered Jo, looking
remorsefully at the golden head, which might have been
swept away from her sight forever under the treacherous ice.

"Quite safe, dear. She is not hurt, and won't even
145 take cold, I think, you were so sensible in covering and
getting her home quickly," replied her mother cheerfully.

Please answer these questions. Look at the passage again if you need to.
You should choose the **best** answer and put a line through its adjacent box.

1

What is meant by 'The storm cleared up' (line 1)?

A The thunder and lightning outside had ended.
B Amy lost her anger as she realised she was in the wrong.
C Everybody in the house was happy once more.
D The argument between the sisters ended with forgiveness.
E The bad weather outside was clearing away the bonfire.

2

'a literary sprout of great promise' (line 5)
Which literary device has been used in this phrase?

A metaphor
B simile
C alliteration
D euphemism
E rhetorical question

3

Which of the following is **not a reason** for Jo's anger?

A Jo had put in a lot of effort into creating her book.
B Jo had gotten rid of her earlier draft of her book.
C Jo had spent years writing this book.
D Jo had put half a dozen fairy tales into the book.
E Jo had felt a deep affection for the stories she had written.

4

Why wasn't the trouble that had occurred discussed before the girls went to bed?

A They did not want Jo to be angry at them as well as Amy.
B They were all angry at Jo for her behaviour towards Amy.
C They all knew it better to let Jo decide when to forgive Amy.
D They all believed that Jo had a right to her anger towards Amy.
E They all knew that Jo would never forgive Amy.

5

What is meant by 'something was wanting' (line 31)?

A There was an absence of hostility and discord.
B Mrs March's voice did not have her usual strength when reading.
C They all wanted to be able to relax and have a happy evening.
D There was a lack of tranquillity and contentment.
E One of the girls desperately wanted something.

PLEASE GO ON TO THE NEXT PAGE

6 'their efforts to be as cheery as larks' (line 35)
Which literary device has been used in this phrase?

A metaphor
B simile
C personification
D alliteration
E contrast

7 What is meant by 'don't let the sun go down upon your anger' (lines 39-40)?

A Do not go to sleep without forgiving the other person first.
B Do not let the end of the day stop you from being enraged.
C Do not be irate when the sun is no longer in the sky.
D Do not let your anger influence your choices.
E None of the above.

8 Why does Jo say that Amy doesn't deserve to be forgiven in a gruff voice?

A Jo's throat was sore from crying.
B Jo wanted her voice to be loud enough for Amy to hear.
C Jo wanted to let Amy know that she was still mad at her.
D Jo wanted her mother to know that she was angry at Amy.
E A & B

9 How does Amy respond to Jo not forgiving her?

A She is displeased that she had not be forgiven.
B She began to regret asking for forgiveness.
C She started to talk about how righteous she had been.
D She became more upset.
E All of the above.

10 Which option best describes Laurie's personality?

A hostile and funny
B jovial and calculating
C sensible and friendly
D good-natured and discouraging
E humorous and timid

PLEASE GO ON TO THE NEXT PAGE

11 Why does Amy want to go to skating?

A because Laurie is going and Amy likes him
B because Jo swore she would take Amy with her
C because she does not want Jo to have fun without her
D because she thinks Jo is a crosspatch
E because Amy wants Jo to forgive her

12 Which group of words best summarise Amy's personality?

A prideful, impatient and short-tempered
B honest, righteous and gentle
C moral, kind and vain
D placid, restless and disgruntled
E impulsive, brave and remorseful

13 Which option best explains why Laurie is 'sounding the ice' (line 85)?

A To test whether they could hear each other across the ice lake.
B The sound the ice makes tells you how long you can skate for.
C In case the hot weather meant that there was no ice at all.
D In case the warm weather had made the ice too thin too skate on.
E To test how fast he and Jo could skate across the ice.

14 'She had cherished her anger till it grew strong and took possession of her' (lines 95-96)
Which literary device has been used in this phrase?

A hyperbole
B simile
C personification
D oxymoron
E alliteration

15 What is the 'little demon she was harbouring' (lines 101-102)?

A pride
B a demon
C jealously
D anger
E grief

PLEASE GO ON TO THE NEXT PAGE

16

Why did Jo stand motionless as Amy crashed through the ice?

A She was still very angry at Amy and so stayed motionless.
B She was terrified of falling through the ice herself.
C She did not know how she could rescue Amy.
D She was waiting for Laurie to come rescue Amy.
E She was held motionless by fear for Amy's life.

17

Which option best describes how Jo and Laurie rescued Amy?

A They used part of the fence to help drag her out.
B They walked her home as quickly as they could.
C They kept her warm by putting their coats on her.
D All of the above.
E A & B

18

Which option best describes why Jo feels remorseful?

A Jo knew that she should have forgiven Amy straight away.
B Amy could have died because Jo was too angry to warn her about the ice.
C Jo had cared more about winning the race than helping Amy.
D Jo knew that she had been in the wrong all along.
E Jo was too scared to help rescue Amy before Laurie had come over.

19

What does 'calamity' (line 12) mean?

A defiance
B catastrophe
C convenience
D accident
E blessing

20

Using the context of the sentence, what does 'plume' (line 54) mean?

A ornament
B beautify
C commend
D feather
E condemn

PLEASE GO ON TO THE NEXT PAGE

21 Which word is **least similar** in meaning to 'exasperating' (line 55)?

A tiring
B frustrating
C delightful
D elegant
E irritating

22 Which word class do the following words belong to?

again (line 41) aloud (line 30) enough (line 8) never (line 12) quite (line 45)

A adverbs
B prepositions
C nouns
D verbs
E adjectives

23 Which of the following words is an abstract noun?

A mourned (line 13)
B stern (line 22)
C kitten (line 13)
D pride (line 4)
E generous (line 27)

24 Which of these is closest in meaning to 'virtuous' (line 62)?

A immoral
B inquisitive
C religious
D meek
E ethical

25 What genre is this text?

A autobiography
B real-life fiction
C mythology
D historical non-fiction
E horror

PLEASE GO ON TO THE NEXT PAGE

In this passage there are some **spelling** mistakes. On each numbered line there is either **one** mistake or **no** mistake. Find the group of words with the mistake in it and mark its letter on your answer sheet. **If there is no mistake, mark N.**

An extract from 'Sense and Sensibility' by Jane Austen

26 Elinor, this eldest daughter, whose advice was so effectual, posessed a strength of

A   B   C   D   N

27 understanding, and coolness of judgemant, which qualified her, though only

A   B   C   D   N

28 nineteen, to be the counselor of her mother. She had an excelent heart; her

A   B   C   D   N

29 disposition was affectionate, and her feelings were strong; but she new how to

A   B   C   D   N

30 govern them: it was a knowlege which one of her sisters had resolved never to be

A   B   C   D   N

31 taught. Marianne's abilitys were, in many respects, quite equal to Elinor's. She was

A   B   C   D   N

32 sensible and clever but eager in everything: her sorows, her joys, could have no

A   B   C   D   N

33 moderation. She was generus, amiable, interesting: she was everything but prudent.

A   B   C   D   N

PLEASE GO ON TO THE NEXT PAGE

In this passage there are some **punctuation and capitalisation** mistakes. On each numbered line there is either **one** mistake or **no** mistake. Find the group of words with the mistake in it and mark its letter on your answer sheet.

Dance With Me

34 "What if nobody will dance with me" whispered Jane anxiously as she persistently
A | B | C | D | N

35 tugged on her older sisters' dress. "Well, I will dance with you," stated Monica,
A | B | C | D | N

36 firmly grabbing Jane's hand Jane gasped in outrage and planted her feet on the
A | B | C | D | N

37 ground "Dance with you? That's too embarrassing!" she shrieked. Monica let go of
A | B | C | D | N

38 Jane's hand— "Then I don't want to dance with you." She paced quickly into the
A | B | C | D | N

39 hall and Jane not wanting to be left alone, hastened after her. Jane started to feel
A | B | C | D | N

40 tears form from watching others having fun dancing. As she was about to leave a
A | B | C | D | N

41 hand grabbed hers. "Lets have some fun!" shouted Monica over the music. Jane
A | B | C | D | N

smiled.

PLEASE GO ON TO THE NEXT PAGE

In this passage you have to choose the **best** word, or **group of words**, to complete each numbered line so that it makes sense and is written in correct English. Choose the **best** answer and mark its letter on your answer sheet.

The Auroras

In Slavic mythology, there are three star

42

gods:	goddess:	goddesses:	god:	demi-gods:
A	B	C	D	E

Morning, Evening and Midnight. They are

43

became	also	becoming	however	yet
A	B	C	D	E

known as The Sisters of the Three Auroras. They help guide the

44

rise	setting	fall	cycle	circle
A	B	C	D	E

of the sun: the Morning Star opens

45

heaven	heavily	heaven's	heavens	havens
A	B	C	D	E

gates for the chariot of the sun to ride

46

though	through	threw	thorough	thoroughly
A	B	C	D	E

in the morning, the Evening Star closes the gates each night

47

during	after	still	with	following
A	B	C	D	E

the sun returns home, and the sun dies in the Midnight Star's arms and

48

was	were	was being	having been	is
A	B	C	D	E

restored to life.

49

Moreover,	However,	Despite this,	Although,	Therefore,
A	B	C	D	E

they also prevent the doomsday dog from devouring the constellation Ursa Minor,

50

who	which	where	what	whom
A	B	C	D	E

would end the universe.

END OF TEST

BLANK PAGE

FIRST PAST THE POST®

English

Multiple-Choice

Test C

Read the following instructions carefully:

1) Do not open this test paper until you are told to do so.

2) Please fill in your details accurately at the top of the answer sheet.

3) Only mark your answer using a **pencil** by drawing a **firm horizontal line** next to your chosen answer on the answer sheet.

4) If you want to change your answer, first rub out your old answer completely and then mark your new answer clearly.

5) Work as efficiently and carefully as you can to ensure you finish within time.

6) If you are unsure of the answer, choose the option you think is the best.

7) When you have finished a page, go straight onto the next page.

8) When you reach the end, go back and check all your answers.

9) This test contains comprehension, spelling, punctuation and grammar questions.

10) There are **50 questions** and you have **50 minutes** in which to complete this paper.

Good luck!

elevenplusexams
head for success

Read this passage carefully, then answer the questions that follow.

Extract from
The Letters of the Right Honourable Lady M--y W--y M--e
Written during Her Travels in Europe, Asia and Africa to Persons of Distinction, Men of Letters, &c. in Different Parts of Europe
by Lady Mary Wortley Montague

Preface

By Mary Astell.

Written in 1724.

I was going, like common editors, to advertise the
5 reader of the beauties and excellencies of the work laid
before him: to tell him, that the illustrious author had
opportunities that other travellers, whatever their quality
or curiosity may have been, cannot obtain; and a genius
capable of making the best improvement of every
10 opportunity. But if the reader, after perusing one letter only
has not discernment to distinguish that natural elegance,
that delicacy of sentiment and observation, that easy
gracefulness, and lovely simplicity, (which is the perfection
of writing) and in which these *Letters* exceed all that has
15 appeared in this kind, or almost in any other, let him lay the
book down, and leave it to those who have.

The noble author had the goodness to lend me her
letters to satisfy my curiosity in some inquiries I had made
concerning her travels; and when I had it in my hands, how
20 was it possible to part with it? I once had the vanity to hope
I might acquaint the public, that it owed this invaluable
treasure to my importunities. But, alas! the most ingenious
author has condemned it to obscurity during her life; and
conviction, as well as deference, obliges me to yield to her
25 reasons. However, if these *Letters* appear hereafter, when I
am in my grave, let this attend them, in testimony to
posterity, that among her contemporaries, one woman, at
least, was just to her merit.

I confess, I am malicious enough to desire, that the
30 world should see to how much better purpose
the LADIES travel than their LORDS; and that, whilst it is
surfeited with Male travels, all in the same tone, and
stuffed with the same trifles; a lady has the skill to strike out
a new path, and to embellish a worn-out subject with a
35 variety of fresh and elegant entertainment. For, besides the
vivacity and spirit which enliven every part, and that
inimitable beauty which spreads through the whole;
besides the purity of the style (for which it may justly be
accounted the standard of the English tongue); the reader
40 will find a more true and accurate account of the customs
and manners of the several nations with whom this lady
conversed, than he can in any other author. But, as her
ladyship's penetration discovers the inmost follies of the
heart, so the candour of her temper passed over them with
45 an air of pity, rather than reproach; treating with the

politeness of a court, and the gentleness of a lady, what the
severity of her judgment could not but condemn.

In short, let her own gender at least, do her justice;
lay aside diabolical Envy, and its brother Malice. Rather let
50 us freely own the superiority, of this sublime genius, as I do,
in the sincerity of my soul; pleased that a woman triumphs,
and proud to follow in her train. Let us offer her the palm
which is so justly her due; and if we pretend to any laurels,
lay them willingly at her feet.

55 LETTER 1.

TO THE COUNTESS OF ——.

Rotterdam, Aug. 3. O. S. 1716.

I flatter myself, dear sister, that I shall give you some
pleasure in letting you know that I have safely passed the
60 sea, though we had the ill fortune of a storm. We were
persuaded by the captain of the yacht to set out in a calm,
and he pretended there was nothing so easy as to tide it
over; but, after two days slowly moving, the wind blew so
hard, that none of the sailors could keep their feet, and we
65 were all Sunday night tossed very handsomely. I never saw a
man more frighted than the captain. For my part, I have
been so lucky, neither to suffer from fear nor seasickness;
though, I confess, I was so impatient to see myself once
more upon dry land, that I would not stay till the yacht could
70 get to Rotterdam, but went in the long-boat to Helvoetsluys,
where we had voitures to carry us to the Briel.

I was charmed with the neatness of that little town;
but my arrival at Rotterdam presented me a new scene of
pleasure. All the streets are paved with broad stones, and
75 before many of the meanest artificers doors are placed
seats of various coloured marbles, so neatly kept, that, I
assure you, I walked almost all over the town
yesterday, incognito, in my slippers without receiving one
spot of dirt; and you may see the Dutch maids washing the
80 pavement of the street, with more application than ours do
our bed-chambers. The town seems so full of people, with
such busy faces, all in motion, that I can hardly fancy it is not
some celebrated fair; but I see it is every day the same. 'Tis
certain no town can be more advantageously situated for
85 commerce. Here are seven large canals, on which the
merchants ships come up to the very doors of their houses.
The shops and warehouses are of a surprising neatness and
magnificence, filled with an incredible quantity of fine

merchandise, and so much cheaper than what we see in
90 England, that I have much ado to persuade myself I am
still so near it. Here is neither dirt nor beggary to be
seen. The common servants, and little shop-women,
here, are more nicely clean than most of our ladies; and
the great variety of neat dresses (every woman dressing
95 her head after her own fashion) is an additional pleasure
in seeing the town.

You see, hitherto, I make no complaints, dear
sister; and if I continue to like travelling as I do at
present, I shall not repent my project. It will go a great
100 way in making me satisfied with it, if it affords me an
opportunity of entertaining you. But it is not from
Holland that you may expect a disinterested offer. I can
write enough in the stile of Rotterdam, to tell you plainly,
in one word that I expect returns of all the London news.
105 You see I have already learnt to make a good bargain;
and that it is not for nothing I will so much as tell you, I
am your affectionate sister.

LET. II
TO MRS. S——.
110   Hague, Aug. 5. O. S. 1716.

I make haste to tell you, dear Madam, that, after
all the dreadful fatigues you threatened me with, I am
hitherto very well pleased with my journey. We take care
to make such short stages every day, that I rather fancy
115 myself upon parties of pleasure, than upon the road; and
sure nothing can be more agreeable than travelling in
Holland. The whole country appears a large garden; the
roads are well paved, shaded on each side with rows of
trees, and bordered with large canals, full of boats,
120 passing and repassing. Every twenty paces gives you the
prospect of some villa, and every four hours that of a
large town, so surprisingly neat, I am sure you would be
charmed with them.

The place I am now at is certainly one of the
125 finest villages in the world. Here are several squares
finely built, and (what I think a particular beauty) the
whole set with thick large trees. The Vour-hout is, at the
same time, the Hyde-Park and Mall of the people of
quality; for they take the air in it both on foot and in
130 coaches. There are shops for wafers, cool liquors, &c.—I
have been to see several of the most celebrated gardens,
but I will not tease you with their descriptions. I dare say
you think my letter already long enough. But I must not
conclude without begging your pardon, for not obeying
135 your commands, in sending the lace you ordered me.
Upon my word, I can yet find none, that is not dearer
than you may buy it at London. If you want any India
goods, here are great variety of penny-worths; and I shall

follow your orders with great pleasure and exactness; being,
140 Dear Madam, &c. &c.

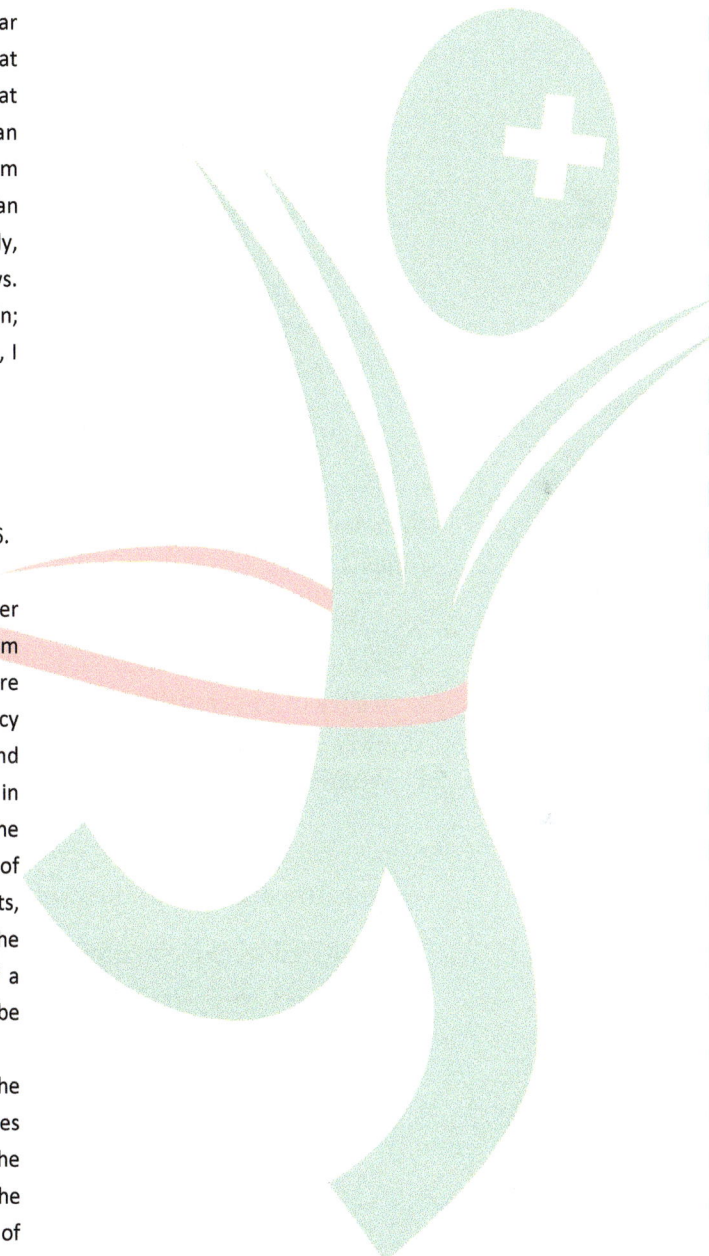

Please answer these questions. Look at the passage again if you need to.
You should choose the **best** answer and put a line through its adjacent box.

1 Which option gives the best definition of 'Preface' (line 1)?

A a title given to a series of letters
B an introduction to a written piece of work
C an advertisement from the narrator
D a monologue describing Mary Astell
E a prepared story to entertain the reader

2 What is meant by 'the reader...has not discernment to distinguish' (lines 10 -16)?

A The reader hasn't got the ability to select the appropriate length of the letters.
B The reader cannot enjoy reading the letters.
C The reader cannot understand the letters.
D The reader hasn't got the ability to judge the letters' quality.
E The reader cannot make negative comparisons between the letters.

3 Which option is **not** one of the qualities Mary Montague is praised for? (lines 11-14)

A pure elegance
B exquisiteness of sentiment
C frailty of observation
D easy gracefulness
E wonderful simplicity

4 What is the purpose of the rhetorical question on lines 19-20?

A For Astell to express how much she enjoyed reading the letters.
B To ask for ways to get rid of the letters.
C To encourage reader to read the letters too.
D A & B
E A & C

5 Which option best explains why Astell could not publish the letters straight away? (lines 22-25)

A Lady Montague didn't edit the letters and so did not want them published.
B The letters were to unclear to be understood by the public.
C Astell did not want to publish the letters while Lady Montague lived.
D Astell wanted to honour Lady Montagu's wishes in regards to the letters.
E Lady Montague forced Astell not to publish the letters.

PLEASE GO ON TO THE NEXT PAGE

6 What does Astell not like about descriptions of travels written by men?

A They are tedious.
B They are uninteresting.
C They all talk about the same subjects.
D They never mention anything new.
E All of the above.

7 Which of the following is **not a reason** why Lady Montague's account is better than a man's? (lines 35-47)

A Her style of writing is pure.
B She enlivens her writing with spirit.
C Her writing is a true and accurate account.
D Her account is written with more pity towards her subjects.
E She has the ability to discover the inmost follies of the heart.

8 What does Astell mean when she writes 'let her own gender at least, do her justice' (line 48)?

A Let men scorn and condemn her for her writings.
B Let men put to right any wrongs done against her.
C Let other women be envious of her accomplishments.
D Let other women praise her and admire her accomplishments.
E B & C

9 What is meant by the phrase 'proud to follow in her train' (line 52)?

A Astell wants to follow Lady Montague's travels on the train.
B Astell wants all women to remain at home and read books.
C Astell wants all women to also aim to triumph over men in their own subjects.
D Astell wants everyone to travel to far off places themselves.
E Astell wants all women to dress the same way that Lady Montague does.

10 Which option best describes how Astell feels about Lady Montague's writing?

A She is proud that such great accounts have been written by a woman.
B She feels that noticing such great writing makes her superior to others.
C She is in awe of Lady Montague's writing.
D A & B
E A & C

PLEASE GO ON TO THE NEXT PAGE

11 What made Lady Montague's journey in the yacht unfortunate?

A The bad storm caused the yacht to be tossed about.
B Lady Montagu was fearful of terrible storms.
C Lady Montagu suffered seasickness during the storm.
D None of the sailors were able to guide the yacht.
E All of the above.

12 Which option is **not a reason** why Lady Montague was charmed with the little town?

A The town was very well-ordered and immaculate.
B There were different shades of marbled seats.
C The town is very busy with people constantly on the move.
D Maids clean the pavements with the same dedication as British ones.
E The merchandise is very lovely.

13 Which option best explains why the town is 'advantageously situated for commerce' (lines 83-85)?

A The town is full of people making it a very busy place.
B They hold a fair every week so the town seems like it is always celebrating.
C The town has seven large canals where merchant ships can come through.
D The shops and warehouses are of a surprising neatness and magnificence.
E The merchandise is much cheaper than the merchandise in England.

14 What does Lady Montague find to be a positive aspect of her travels? (lines 97-107)

A She can amuse her sister with tales of her travels.
B She has grasped how to make a fine bargain.
C She can expect to hear all the gossip and news from London.
D all of the above
E A & B

15 Which option does Lady Montagu **not say** makes her journey pleasant? (lines 101-125)

A They can see beautiful scenery of Holland.
B Holding parties of pleasure on their journey.
C Going only a short distance every day.
D The roads are built well.
E There are very fine and beautiful towns.

PLEASE GO ON TO THE NEXT PAGE

16 Why can't Lady Montague fulfil the recipient's request? (lines 135-137)

    A She has found some lace but it is too expensive to buy.
    B She can't find any lace on her travels that is nicer than the lace in London.
    C She can't find the exact amount of lace that is needed by the recipient.
    D She has found some lace, but it is much too cheap.
    E She cannot find any lace to send to the recipient.

17 Which of the following statements are true? The two letters were written...

    A from Rotterdam on August 30th 1716 and Hague on August 5th 1716.
    B from England August 1st 1716 and Hague August 16th 1750.
    C from Rotterdam on August 3rd 1716 and Hague on August 5th 1716.
    D from Hague Spring 1716 and Rotterdam Summer 1716.
    E from Rotterdam on August 17th 1716 and Hague on August 15th 1716.

18 Which group of words best describe Lady Montague's personality?

    A bold, sly, pessimistic
    B triumphant, caring, apprehensive
    C dynamic, daring, pathetic
    D opportunistic, malicious, timid
    E adventurous, generous, spirited

19 What does 'obscurity' (line 23) mean?

    A mystery
    B anonymity
    C death
    D renown
    E importance

20 Which of these is **least similar** in meaning to 'vivacity' (line 36)?

    A liveliness
    B cleverness
    C regret
    D animation
    E indifference

PLEASE GO ON TO THE NEXT PAGE

21 Which literary device has been used in the following line?

'lay aside diabolical Envy, and its brother Malice' (line 49)

A alliteration
B simile
C personification
D rhetorical question
E hyperbole

22 What type of words are the following?

haste (line 111) fatigues (line 112) exactness (line 139)

pardon (line 134)   complaints (line 97)

A adverbs
B prepositions
C nouns
D verbs
E adjectives

23 What does 'handsomely' (line 65) mean?

A attractively
B smartly
C slowly
D thoroughly
E colourfully

24 Which of the following is an adverb?

A flatter (line 58)
B hitherto (line 97)
C charmed (line 123)
D merit (line 28)
E neatness (line 72)

25 What genre does this text belong to?

A fantasy
B non-fiction
C science fiction
D mystery
E thriller

PLEASE GO ON TO THE NEXT PAGE

In this passage there are some **spelling** mistakes. On each numbered line there is either **one** mistake or **no** mistake. Find the group of words with the mistake in it and mark its letter on your answer sheet. **If there is no mistake, mark N.**

An extract from 'The Picture of Dorian Gray' by Oscar Wilde

26 The artist is the creator of beautiful things. To reveal art and conceal the artist is

A　　　B　　　C　　　D　　　N

27 art's aim. The critic is he who can translate into another maner or a new material

A　　　B　　　C　　　D　　　N

28 his impresion of beautiful things. The highest, as the lowest, form of criticism is a

A　　　B　　　C　　　D　　　N

29 mode of autobiograpy. Those who find ugly meanings in beautiful things are corrupt

A　　　B　　　C　　　D　　　N

30 without being charming. This is a falt. Those who find beautiful meanings in beautiful

A　　　B　　　C　　　D　　　N

31 things are the cultivated. For these, there is hope. They are the elect to whom

A　　　B　　　C　　　D　　　N

32 beautiful things mean only beauty. There is no such thing as a moral or an ummoral

A　　　B　　　C　　　D　　　N

33 book. Books are well written, or badly written. That is all. The artist can expres

A　　　B　　　C　　　D　　　N

everything.

PLEASE GO ON TO THE NEXT PAGE

In these sentences there are some **punctuation and capitalisation** mistakes. On each numbered line there is either **one** mistake or **no** mistake. Find the group of words with the mistake in it and mark its letter on your answer sheet. **If there is no mistake, mark N.**

Colours

34 Her eyes are blue; they were as blue as the crashing roaring sea on a stormy day.

A   B   C   D   N

35 His hair is so golden and shiny; its as if the sun had created a halo around his head.

A   B   C   D   N

36 The necklaces jewel stones lightened to an enchanting lavender under the water.

A   B   C   D   N

37 The sky was filled with ominous clouds, which were a dreary grey and the rain fell.

A   B   C   D   N

38 Everyone was amazed by May's spectacular hair, she had dyed it a dazzling violet.

A   B   C   D   N

39 She couldnt believe what she was seeing; the ocean had just become bright green!

A   B   C   D   N

40 Can you imagine anything more gloriously beautiful than the colours in a rainbow.

A   B   C   D   N

41 He was charmed by the contrasting light and dark shades in Salvador dali's painting.

A   B   C   D   N

PLEASE GO ON TO THE NEXT PAGE

In this passage you have to choose the **best** word, or **group of words**, to complete each numbered line so that it makes sense and is written in correct English. Choose the **best** answer and mark its letter on your answer sheet.

The Sketch

My fingerprints

42

smudge	smudges	smudged	smudging	will smudge
A	B	C	D	E

the corners of the paper as I go to clip it to the washing line. I

43

see	look	understand	saw	turn
A	B	C	D	E

at the drawing to assess any differences it has to the face in the mirror.

44

By	At	As	To	With
A	B	C	D	E

careful consideration, I mark the key highlights of my features. If I succeed, this all will

45

having been	being	been	have been	had been
A	B	C	D	E

worth all the countless hours I spent obsessing

46

over	onto	across	because of	at
A	B	C	D	E

the page with my pencil. However, to achieve my goal, these key points

47

could	might	must	can	may
A	B	C	D	E

match those in the sketch. I hold my breath as I

48

careful	care	carefulness	carefully	carelessly
A	B	C	D	E

compare my face with the accentuated features of the picture.

49

I	My	We	Mine	Your
A	B	C	D	E

heart stops for a beat. "Yes!!!" I

50

state	say	shouted	said	shout
A	B	C	D	E

out loud for all to hear.

END OF TEST

BLANK PAGE

FIRST PAST THE POST®

English

Multiple-Choice

Test D

Read the following instructions carefully:

1) Do not open this test paper until you are told to do so.

2) Please fill in your details accurately at the top of the answer sheet.

3) Only mark your answer using a **pencil** by drawing a **firm horizontal line** next to your chosen answer on the answer sheet.

4) If you want to change your answer, first rub out your old answer completely and then mark your new answer clearly.

5) Work as efficiently and carefully as you can to ensure you finish within time.

6) If you are unsure of the answer, choose the option you think is the best.

7) When you have finished a page, go straight onto the next page.

8) When you reach the end, go back and check all your answers.

9) This test contains comprehension, spelling, punctuation and grammar questions.

10) There are **50 questions** and you have **50 minutes** in which to complete this paper.

Good luck!

elevenplusexams
head for success

Read this passage carefully, then answer the questions that follow.

The Cloud
by Percy Bysshe Shelley

I bring fresh showers for the thirsting flowers,
From the seas and the streams;
I bear light shade for the leaves when laid
In their noonday dreams.
5   From my wings are shaken the dews that waken
The sweet buds every one,
When rocked to rest on their mother's breast,
As she dances about the sun.
I wield the flail of the lashing hail,
10 And whiten the green plains under,
And then again I dissolve it in rain,
And laugh as I pass in thunder.

I sift the snow on the mountains below,
And their great pines groan aghast;
15 And all the night 'tis my pillow white,
While I sleep in the arms of the blast.
Sublime on the towers of my skiey bowers,
Lightning my pilot sits;
In a cavern under is fettered the thunder,
20 It struggles and howls at fits;
Over earth and ocean, with gentle motion,
This pilot is guiding me,
Lured by the love of the genii that move
In the depths of the purple sea;
25 Over the rills, and the crags, and the hills,
Over the lakes and the plains,
Wherever he dream, under mountain or stream,
The Spirit he loves remains;
And I all the while bask in Heaven's blue smile,
30 Whilst he is dissolving in rains.

The sanguine Sunrise, with his meteor eyes,
And his burning plumes outspread,
Leaps on the back of my sailing rack,
When the morning star shines dead;
35 As on the jag of a mountain crag,
Which an earthquake rocks and swings,
An eagle alit one moment may sit
In the light of its golden wings.
And when Sunset may breathe, from the lit sea beneath,
40 Its ardours of rest and of love,
And the crimson pall of eve may fall
From the depth of Heaven above,
With wings folded I rest, on mine aëry nest,

As still as a brooding dove.

45 That orbèd maiden with white fire laden,
Whom mortals call the Moon,
Glides glimmering o'er my fleece-like floor,
By the midnight breezes strewn;
And wherever the beat of her unseen feet,
50 Which only the angels hear,
May have broken the woof of my tent's thin roof,
The stars peep behind her and peer;
And I laugh to see them whirl and flee,
Like a swarm of golden bees,
55 When I widen the rent in my wind-built tent,
Till calm the rivers, lakes, and seas,
Like strips of the sky fallen through me on high,
Are each paved with the moon and these.

I bind the Sun's throne with a burning zone,
60 And the Moon's with a girdle of pearl;
The volcanoes are dim, and the stars reel and swim,
When the whirlwinds my banner unfurl.
From cape to cape, with a bridge-like shape,
Over a torrent sea,
65 Sunbeam-proof, I hang like a roof,
The mountains its columns be.
The triumphal arch through which I march
With hurricane, fire, and snow,
When the Powers of the air are chained to my chair,
70 Is the million-coloured bow;
The sphere-fire above its soft colours wove,
While the moist Earth was laughing below.

I am the daughter of Earth and Water,
And the nursling of the Sky;
75 I pass through the pores of the ocean and shores;
I change, but I cannot die.
For after the rain when with never a stain
The pavilion of Heaven is bare,
And the winds and sunbeams with their convex gleams
80 Build up the blue dome of air,
I silently laugh at my own cenotaph,
And out of the caverns of rain,
Like a child from the womb, like a ghost from the tomb,
I arise and unbuild it again.

Please answer these questions. Look at the passage again if you need to.
You should choose the **best** answer and put a line through its adjacent box.

1   Which rhyme scheme is used in the first four lines of stanza one?

A   ABCD
B   ABBC
C   ABCB
D   AABB
E   ACBC

2   Which of the following options is **not true** about the Cloud in the first stanza?

A   It brings rain from the streams and oceans.
B   The cloud casts a shade over the leaves.
C   The cloud dances beneath the sun.
D   The cloud hurls down hailstones that whiten the fields.
E   It provides water for the fading flowers.

3   How do the mountains' pines feel about the snow? (lines 13-15)

A   appalled
B   cautious
C   craven
D   adventurous
E   content

4   Which option best describes how the lightning acts differently from the thunder in stanza two?
A   The lightning is more malicious than the thunder.
B   The lightning is more tender than the thunder.
C   The lightning is more powerful than the thunder.
D   A & B
E   B & C

5   What controls the Cloud's movement in stanza two?

A   Thunder
B   Lightning
C   the blast
D   A & B
E   B & C

PLEASE GO ON TO THE NEXT PAGE

6 What does the repetition of the word 'over' in stanza two emphasise?

A how high the cloud floats.
B how the Lightning feels it is superior to the earth.
C how brightly the Lightning flashes across a variety of different places.
D how the Cloud travels across a vast amount of places.
E how few places the Spirit chooses to dwell.

7 What is meant by 'I all the while bask in Heaven's blue smile' (line 29)?

A The Cloud waits for the lightning to clear and the blue sky to appear.
B Whilst the lightning flashes, the Cloud dies in the comfort of the blue sky.
C The Spirit escapes the lightning by hiding within the warmth of the blue sky.
D The Cloud savours being within the benevolence of the blue sky.
E The Cloud dreams of being under the affectionate blue sky.

8 'As on the jag of a mountain crag' (line 35)
Which literary device is being used in this line?

A personification
B metaphor
C onomatopoeia
D hyperbole
E assonance

9 Which of the following options is a **true** statement from stanza three?

A The Sunrise's rays coiled inwards.
B The sea darkens as the sun sets.
C A golden eagle sits upon the mountain crag all morning.
D The Sun's light can still be seen after it has set.
E The Cloud is heavy with rain.

10 What does the following simile tell us about the Cloud?
'With wings folded I rest, on mine aëry nest/As still as a brooding dove.' (lines 43-44)

A The Cloud is getting ready to release its rain upon the earth.
B The Cloud, at this moment, has a contrasting personality to the sun.
C The Cloud is light, intangible and feels peaceful.
D The Cloud is preparing a place where it can sleep.
E The Cloud is bulky and is feeling apprehensive.

PLEASE GO ON TO THE NEXT PAGE

11 Which of the following **incorrectly** describes the poem's mood from stanza two to stanza three?

A   Stanza three creates a less hostile mood.
B   Stanza three establishes a more tranquil mood.
C   Stanza three creates a more joyful mood.
D   Stanza two establishes a more energetic mood.
E   Stanza three has a more passionate mood.

12 Which option best describes the Moon in stanza four?

A   The Moon is spherical, celestial, female and shines with a fierce white light.
B   The Moon is round, mortal, female and shines with a subdued white light.
C   The Moon is oval, immortal, male and glows with an intense white light.
D   The Moon is lifeless, spherical and glows with a bright white light.
E   The Moon is a circular, eternal and shines with a fierce silver light.

13 What does the following alliteration emphasise about the movement of the Moon?
'Glides glimmering' (line 47)

A   how the Moon glitters when it travels over the Cloud.
B   how soft the Cloud appears when the Moon travels over it.
C   how the Moon travels smoothly and gently over the Cloud.
D   how brightly the Moon is shining over the Cloud.
E   how quickly and powerfully the Moon is moving over the Cloud.

14 What is being described in the following line?
'the beat of her unseen feet'? (line 49)

A   the sound that the Moon makes
B   the Moon's rays of light
C   how the Moon walks on the earth
D   how heavy the Moon is
E   the way in which people react to the Moon's music

15 Which option best explains why 'the moist Earth was laughing' (line 72)?

A   The Earth was laughing cruelly at how arrogant the Cloud was acting.
B   The Earth was laughing in awe at all the rain the Cloud could generate.
C   The Earth was laughing pitilessly at the amount of work the Cloud had to do.
D   The Earth was laughing in wonder and joy at the rainbow the Cloud created.
E   The Earth was laughing at the Cloud for finding joy in creating a rainbow.

PLEASE GO ON TO THE NEXT PAGE

16 Which of the following statements about the Cloud is untrue? (lines 73– 84)

A The Cloud is immortal.
B The Cloud is the mother of the sky.
C The Cloud demolishes the blue skies.
D The Cloud rebuilds itself from the water it generates.
E The Cloud is constantly changing its shape and form.

17 Which option best describes the Cloud's personality?

A powerful, despondent, sympathetic
B benevolent, mischievous, weak
C whimsical, inconstant, influential
D humane, malicious, exuberant
E considerate, inquisitive, solid

18 Which option best describes how the narrator wants us to feel about the Cloud?

A He wants us to think of the Cloud positively; something that brings life joy.
B He wants us to be feel indifferent towards the Cloud; it is neither good nor bad.
C He wants us to think of the Cloud negatively; something to be feared.
D He want us to think of the Cloud as having great power over our lives.
E A & D

19 What does 'fettered' (line 19) mean?

A screeched
B slept
C infused
D constrained
E threatened

20 Which of these is **least similar** in meaning to 'sanguine' (line 31)?

A optimistic
B assured
C melancholy
D impractical
E cheerful

PLEASE GO ON TO THE NEXT PAGE

21 What does 'rent' (line 55) mean?

A   burden
B   hire
C   levy
D   lease
E   rupture

22 Which of the following words is not a verb?

A   peep (line 52)
B   peer (line 52)
C   through (line 57)
D   flee (line 53)
E   whirl (line 53)

23 Which word class characterises the following?

burning (line 59)   dim (line 61)   torrent (line 64)

triumphal (line 67)   soft (line 71)

A   nouns
B   verbs
C   adverbs
D   adjectives
E   prepositions

24 Which of the following is an adverb?

A   convex (line 79)
B   never (line 77)
C   pavilion (line 78)
D   cenotaph (line 81)
E   gleams (line 79)

25 What literary device is used consistently throughout the entire poem?

A   simile
B   hyperbole
C   metaphor
D   personification
E   euphemism

PLEASE GO ON TO THE NEXT PAGE

In this passage there are some **spelling** mistakes. On each numbered line there is either **one** mistake or **no** mistake. Find the group of words with the mistake in it and mark its letter on your answer sheet. **If there is no mistake, mark N.**

An extract from 'Jane Eyre' by Charlotte Bronte

26 It was a fine, calm day, though very cold; I was tired of siting still in the library
A   B   C   D   N

27 through a hole long morning: Mrs. Fairfax had just written a letter which was
A   B   C   D   N

28 waiting to be posted, so I put on my bonnet and cloak and voluntered to carry it to
A   B   C   D   N

29 Hay; the distance, two miles, would be a pleasent winter afternoon walk. The
A   B   C   D   N

30 ground was hard, the air was still, my road was lonly; I walked fast till I got warm,
A   B   C   D   N

31 and then I walked slowly to enjoy and analyse the species of pleasure brooding for
A   B   C   D   N

32 me in the hour and situation. It was three o'clock; the church bell tolled as I pased
A   B   C   D   N

33 under the belfry: the charm of the hour lay in its aproaching dimness, in the low-
A   B   C   D   N

gliding and pale-beaming sun.

PLEASE GO ON TO THE NEXT PAGE

In these sentences there are some **punctuation and capitalisation** mistakes. On each numbered line there is either **one** mistake or **no** mistake. Find the group of words with the mistake in it and mark its letter on your answer sheet. **If there is no mistake, mark N.**

Owls

34 It is quite rare to see an owl: most owls are either nocturnal or crepuscular (active

A   B   C   D   N

35 at dawn and dusk. They are specialised birds with round heads and rather flat or

A   B   C   D   N

36 dished faces, with forward-facing eyes and a short, hooked bill these features

A   B   C   D   N

37 help owls to hunt and catch their prey, which they need, because they are

A   B   C   D   N

38 carnivores. For example, owls eyes have adapted to hunting in the dark by

A   B   C   D   N

39 becoming very large. so as to give their eyes a large surface area to collect light,

A   B   C   D   N

40 which helps them to see in low light levels. Moreover to aid them in catching their

A   B   C   D   N

41 prey, owls have also adapted their wings to: form a special edge on the front of

A   B   C   D   N

their wings that breaks air into small streams of wind to give them almost silent flight.

PLEASE GO ON TO THE NEXT PAGE

In these sentences you have to choose the **best** word, or **group of words**, to complete each numbered line so that it makes sense and is written in correct English. Choose the **best** answer and mark its letter on your answer sheet.

A Series of Unfortunate Weather Conditions

There were no umbrellas on the beach

42

who	what	because	which	so
A	B	C	D	E

could provide us shade from the blistering sun.

I was excited about the upcoming match,

43

although	however	moreover	also	similarly
A	B	C	D	E

the rain threatened to cancel the game.

I was soaking wet

44

because	except	so	then	therefore
A	B	C	D	E

it was raining cats and dogs outside and I had forgotten my raincoat.

It was so

45

warmth	cold	tepid	hot	chilly
A	B	C	D	E

today that I felt like an ice cream left out too long in the sun.

I had

46

few	couple	several	short	deep
A	B	C	D	E

tiny bruises from the hailstones that had suddenly pelted down upon me.

47

Moreover,	Although,	Despite	However,	Also,
A	B	C	D	E

the fact that it was bright and sunny outside, I had to spend the entire day indoors.

We

48

was	will be	would be	were	had been
A	B	C	D	E

freezing tomorrow when it starts to snow.

Due to the frozen ice, I had

49

got	gotten	get	getting	gets
A	B	C	D	E

a very bad bruise when I had fallen over.

The strong winds help to create the

50

strongest	strong	slightest	large	heaviest
A	B	C	D	E

storm this area has seen in over fifty years.

END OF TEST

FIRST PAST THE POST®

Answer Sheets

English: Practice Papers

Multiple Choice
Book 2

FIRST PAST THE POST SERIES BY ELEVENPLUSEXAMS

Pupil's Name

School Name

Date of Test / /

ENGLISH: TEST A

Answer like this ▭

PUPIL NUMBER

[0]	[0]	[0]	[0]	[0]	[0]
[1]	[1]	[1]	[1]	[1]	[1]
[2]	[2]	[2]	[2]	[2]	[2]
[3]	[3]	[3]	[3]	[3]	[3]
[4]	[4]	[4]	[4]	[4]	[4]
[5]	[5]	[5]	[5]	[5]	[5]
[6]	[6]	[6]	[6]	[6]	[6]
[7]	[7]	[7]	[7]	[7]	[7]
[8]	[8]	[8]	[8]	[8]	[8]

EXAM CENTRE

[0]	[0]	[0]	[0]	[0]	[0]	[0]
[1]	[1]	[1]	[1]	[1]	[1]	[1]
[2]	[2]	[2]	[2]	[2]	[2]	[2]
[3]	[3]	[3]	[3]	[3]	[3]	[3]
[4]	[4]	[4]	[4]	[4]	[4]	[4]
[5]	[5]	[5]	[5]	[5]	[5]	[5]
[6]	[6]	[6]	[6]	[6]	[6]	[6]
[7]	[7]	[7]	[7]	[7]	[7]	[7]

DATE OF BIRTH

Day	Month	Year
[0] [0]	January	2007
[1] [1]	February	2008
[2] [2]	March	2009
[3] [3]	April	2010
[4]	May	2011
[5]	June	2012
[6]	July	2013
[7]	August	2014
[8]	September	2015
[9]	October	2016
	November	2017
	December	2018

Villain?

1 A B C D E
2 A B C D E
3 A B C D E
4 A B C D E
5 A B C D E
6 A B C D E
7 A B C D E

8 A B C D E
9 A B C D E
10 A B C D E
11 A B C D E
12 A B C D E
13 A B C D E
14 A B C D E

15 A B C D E
16 A B C D E
17 A B C D E
18 A B C D E
19 A B C D E
20 A B C D E
21 A B C D E

22 A B C D E
23 A B C D E
24 A B C D E
25 A B C D E

Monsters & Heroes

26 A B C D N
27 A B C D N
28 A B C D N
29 A B C D N
30 A B C D N
31 A B C D N
32 A B C D N
33 A B C D N

The Brothers Grimm

34	35	36	37	38	39	40	41
A ▭	A ▭	A ▭	A ▭	A ▭	A ▭	A ▭	A ▭
B ▭	B ▭	B ▭	B ▭	B ▭	B ▭	B ▭	B ▭
C ▭	C ▭	C ▭	C ▭	C ▭	C ▭	C ▭	C ▭
D ▭	D ▭	D ▭	D ▭	D ▭	D ▭	D ▭	D ▭
N ▭	N ▭	N ▭	N ▭	N ▭	N ▭	N ▭	N ▭

A Good Fairy Point of View

42	43	44	45	46	47	48
A ▭	A ▭	A ▭	A ▭	A ▭	A ▭	A ▭
B ▭	B ▭	B ▭	B ▭	B ▭	B ▭	B ▭
C ▭	C ▭	C ▭	C ▭	C ▭	C ▭	C ▭
D ▭	D ▭	D ▭	D ▭	D ▭	D ▭	D ▭
E ▭	E ▭	E ▭	E ▭	E ▭	E ▭	E ▭

49	50
A ▭	A ▭
B ▭	B ▭
C ▭	C ▭
D ▭	D ▭
E ▭	E ▭

Pupil's Name

School Name

Date of Test / /

ENGLISH: TEST B

Answer like this ▬

PUPIL NUMBER

[0]	[0]	[0]	[0]	[0]	[0]
[1]	[1]	[1]	[1]	[1]	[1]
[2]	[2]	[2]	[2]	[2]	[2]
[3]	[3]	[3]	[3]	[3]	[3]
[4]	[4]	[4]	[4]	[4]	[4]
[5]	[5]	[5]	[5]	[5]	[5]
[6]	[6]	[6]	[6]	[6]	[6]
[7]	[7]	[7]	[7]	[7]	[7]
[8]	[8]	[8]	[8]	[8]	[8]

EXAM CENTRE

[0]	[0]	[0]	[0]	[0]	[0]	[0]
[1]	[1]	[1]	[1]	[1]	[1]	[1]
[2]	[2]	[2]	[2]	[2]	[2]	[2]
[3]	[3]	[3]	[3]	[3]	[3]	[3]
[4]	[4]	[4]	[4]	[4]	[4]	[4]
[5]	[5]	[5]	[5]	[5]	[5]	[5]
[6]	[6]	[6]	[6]	[6]	[6]	[6]
[7]	[7]	[7]	[7]	[7]	[7]	[7]

DATE OF BIRTH

Day	Month	Year
[0] [0]	January	2007
[1] [1]	February	2008
[2] [2]	March	2009
[3] [3]	April	2010
[4]	May	2011
[5]	June	2012
[6]	July	2013
[7]	August	2014
[8]	September	2015
[9]	October	2016
	November	2017
	December	2018

Little Women

Questions 1–25, each with options A, B, C, D, E.

1	2	3	4	5	6	7
8	9	10	11	12	13	14
15	16	17	18	19	20	21
22	23	24	25			

Sense and Sensibility

Questions 26–33, each with options A, B, C, D, N.

| 26 | 27 | 28 | 29 | 30 | 31 | 32 | 33 |

ENGLISH: TEST B

Dance with Me

34	35	36	37	38	39	40	41
A ▭	A ▭	A ▭	A ▭	A ▭	A ▭	A ▭	A ▭
B ▭	B ▭	B ▭	B ▭	B ▭	B ▭	B ▭	B ▭
C ▭	C ▭	C ▭	C ▭	C ▭	C ▭	C ▭	C ▭
D ▭	D ▭	D ▭	D ▭	D ▭	D ▭	D ▭	D ▭
N ▭	N ▭	N ▭	N ▭	N ▭	N ▭	N ▭	N ▭

The Auroras

42	43	44	45	46	47	48
A ▭	A ▭	A ▭	A ▭	A ▭	A ▭	A ▭
B ▭	B ▭	B ▭	B ▭	B ▭	B ▭	B ▭
C ▭	C ▭	C ▭	C ▭	C ▭	C ▭	C ▭
D ▭	D ▭	D ▭	D ▭	D ▭	D ▭	D ▭
E ▭	E ▭	E ▭	E ▭	E ▭	E ▭	E ▭

49	50
A ▭	A ▭
B ▭	B ▭
C ▭	C ▭
D ▭	D ▭
E ▭	E ▭

Pupil's Name

School Name

Date of Test   / /

ENGLISH: TEST C

Answer like this ▬

PUPIL NUMBER

[0]	[0]	[0]	[0]	[0]	[0]
[1]	[1]	[1]	[1]	[1]	[1]
[2]	[2]	[2]	[2]	[2]	[2]
[3]	[3]	[3]	[3]	[3]	[3]
[4]	[4]	[4]	[4]	[4]	[4]
[5]	[5]	[5]	[5]	[5]	[5]
[6]	[6]	[6]	[6]	[6]	[6]
[7]	[7]	[7]	[7]	[7]	[7]
[8]	[8]	[8]	[8]	[8]	[8]

EXAM CENTRE

[0]	[0]	[0]	[0]	[0]	[0]	[0]
[1]	[1]	[1]	[1]	[1]	[1]	[1]
[2]	[2]	[2]	[2]	[2]	[2]	[2]
[3]	[3]	[3]	[3]	[3]	[3]	[3]
[4]	[4]	[4]	[4]	[4]	[4]	[4]
[5]	[5]	[5]	[5]	[5]	[5]	[5]
[6]	[6]	[6]	[6]	[6]	[6]	[6]
[7]	[7]	[7]	[7]	[7]	[7]	[7]

DATE OF BIRTH

Day	Month	Year
[0] [0]	January	2007
[1] [1]	February	2008
[2] [2]	March	2009
[3] [3]	April	2010
[4]	May	2011
[5]	June	2012
[6]	July	2013
[7]	August	2014
[8]	September	2015
[9]	October	2016
	November	2017
	December	2018

The Letters of the Right Honourable Lady M--y W--y M--e

1 A B C D E
2 A B C D E
3 A B C D E
4 A B C D E
5 A B C D E
6 A B C D E
7 A B C D E

8 A B C D E
9 A B C D E
10 A B C D E
11 A B C D E
12 A B C D E
13 A B C D E
14 A B C D E

15 A B C D E
16 A B C D E
17 A B C D E
18 A B C D E
19 A B C D E
20 A B C D E
21 A B C D E

22 A B C D E
23 A B C D E
24 A B C D E
25 A B C D E

The Picture of Dorian Gray

26 A B C D N
27 A B C D N
28 A B C D N
29 A B C D N
30 A B C D N
31 A B C D N
32 A B C D N
33 A B C D N

Colours

34	35	36	37	38	39	40	41
A ☐	A ☐	A ☐	A ☐	A ☐	A ☐	A ☐	A ☐
B ☐	B ☐	B ☐	B ☐	B ☐	B ☐	B ☐	B ☐
C ☐	C ☐	C ☐	C ☐	C ☐	C ☐	C ☐	C ☐
D ☐	D ☐	D ☐	D ☐	D ☐	D ☐	D ☐	D ☐
N ☐	N ☐	N ☐	N ☐	N ☐	N ☐	N ☐	N ☐

The Sketch

42	43	44	45	46	47	48
A ☐	A ☐	A ☐	A ☐	A ☐	A ☐	A ☐
B ☐	B ☐	B ☐	B ☐	B ☐	B ☐	B ☐
C ☐	C ☐	C ☐	C ☐	C ☐	C ☐	C ☐
D ☐	D ☐	D ☐	D ☐	D ☐	D ☐	D ☐
E ☐	E ☐	E ☐	E ☐	E ☐	E ☐	E ☐

49	50
A ☐	A ☐
B ☐	B ☐
C ☐	C ☐
D ☐	D ☐
E ☐	E ☐

Pupil's Name

School Name

Date of Test / /

ENGLISH: TEST D

Answer like this ▬

PUPIL NUMBER

[0]	[0]	[0]	[0]	[0]	[0]
[1]	[1]	[1]	[1]	[1]	[1]
[2]	[2]	[2]	[2]	[2]	[2]
[3]	[3]	[3]	[3]	[3]	[3]
[4]	[4]	[4]	[4]	[4]	[4]
[5]	[5]	[5]	[5]	[5]	[5]
[6]	[6]	[6]	[6]	[6]	[6]
[7]	[7]	[7]	[7]	[7]	[7]
[8]	[8]	[8]	[8]	[8]	[8]

EXAM CENTRE

[0]	[0]	[0]	[0]	[0]	[0]	[0]
[1]	[1]	[1]	[1]	[1]	[1]	[1]
[2]	[2]	[2]	[2]	[2]	[2]	[2]
[3]	[3]	[3]	[3]	[3]	[3]	[3]
[4]	[4]	[4]	[4]	[4]	[4]	[4]
[5]	[5]	[5]	[5]	[5]	[5]	[5]
[6]	[6]	[6]	[6]	[6]	[6]	[6]
[7]	[7]	[7]	[7]	[7]	[7]	[7]

DATE OF BIRTH

Day	Month		Year	
[0]	[0]	January	2007	
[1]	[1]	February	2008	
[2]	[2]	March	2009	
[3]	[3]	April	2010	
	[4]	May	2011	
	[5]	June	2012	
	[6]	July	2013	
	[7]	August	2014	
	[8]	September	2015	
	[9]	October	2016	
		November	2017	
		December	2018	

The Cloud

Questions 1–25: each has options A, B, C, D, E.

Jane Eyre

Questions 26–33: each has options A, B, C, D, N.

Owls

34	35	36	37	38	39	40	41
A ▢	A ▢	A ▢	A ▢	A ▢	A ▢	A ▢	A ▢
B ▢	B ▢	B ▢	B ▢	B ▢	B ▢	B ▢	B ▢
C ▢	C ▢	C ▢	C ▢	C ▢	C ▢	C ▢	C ▢
D ▢	D ▢	D ▢	D ▢	D ▢	D ▢	D ▢	D ▢
N ▢	N ▢	N ▢	N ▢	N ▢	N ▢	N ▢	N ▢

A Series of Unfortunate Weather Conditions

42	43	44	45	46	47	48
A ▢	A ▢	A ▢	A ▢	A ▢	A ▢	A ▢
B ▢	B ▢	B ▢	B ▢	B ▢	B ▢	B ▢
C ▢	C ▢	C ▢	C ▢	C ▢	C ▢	C ▢
D ▢	D ▢	D ▢	D ▢	D ▢	D ▢	D ▢
E ▢	E ▢	E ▢	E ▢	E ▢	E ▢	E ▢

49	50
A ▢	A ▢
B ▢	B ▢
C ▢	C ▢
D ▢	D ▢
E ▢	E ▢

BLANK PAGE

Answers & Explanations
English: Practice Papers

Multiple Choice
Book 2

ENGLISH: TEST A

Question	Answer	Explanation
1	C	Entire Text: The fairy tale must involve an Evil Stepmother who has two daughters and the text quotes that Ana wants the girl to sweep up the 'cinders' (line 128).
2	C	Text (lines 9-16): The constant repetition of the word 'one' is to keep showing the reader that Clara is always first to do anything and so always comes first in their parents' eyes.
3	C	Text (lines 10-16): 'Clara walked one second before her, learned to read one month before her... she could dance more gracefully, flirt more subtly and make her dresses look one monumental touch prettier.' Gracefully is a synonym of elegantly.
4	A	Text (line 21-24): 'and Ana who was to be Clara's background support by increasing the Tremaine family's steadily growing, reputable wealth by marrying the richest local grocer.'
5	A	Text (lines 29-32): From these two paragraphs, we know that Ana grows in 'skill, intelligence and maliciousness' in her determination to find her own husband. Canny and intelligent are synonyms, and hostile and malicious are synonyms.
6	E	Text (lines 34-36): 'Married to a simple but kind and wealthy man, with enough rank to release Ana from the clutches of jealousy and the greedy, grasping hands of her parents.' When the narrator talks of rank, they are talking about his position in society and we know from the text that Ana's parents wanted Ana to marry a wealthy husband.
7	C	Text (lines 37-42): '...she had two precious daughters, Drizella and Anastasia ...all-consuming love Ana felt for her two most beloved jewels... '. The jewels Ana is referring to are her two daughters.
8	B	Text (lines 48-52): 'Most of all, Ana...ensured that both her daughters were treated, as equals in everything they undertook and in everything they received.'
9	A	Text (lines 74-76): '...(he was of a more modest income) ... (being merely a gentleman who made his money from trade), ' This information tells us more about Sir Traver's rank in society— he didn't have a very high position in society.
10	D	Text (lines 78-86): 'He willingly and delightedly spent time with them... '. He was not pretending to be happy to spend time with Ana's daughters.
11	D	Text (lines 110-113): As the air is now 'gloomy' and 'cold', Ana must be feeling sad (anguished) and she must feel distant and angry towards her husband as she is offended (displeased) by his behaviour.
12	D	Text (lines 115-123): '...she felt the return of some old friends ...Ana felt her jealousy and hatred grow again from the seed planted long ago.'
13	E	Text (lines 124-126): 'She had never felt such despair watching her own daughters suffering the cruelty her parents had inflicted upon her.' We know from the beginning of the text that the cruelty Ana describes is the favouring of one child over another.'
14	C	Text (lines 135-138): 'Ana would never answer to the moniker of the 'Evil Stepmother'. However, she would always, always claim the name of 'Mother'.' The repetition shows that Ana fully believes that her actions were right because those actions were for her daughters.
15	B	Text (lines 3-4): 'Impress' in this context means 'to mark' and 'epithet' means 'title'.
16	C	Text (lines 6-7): There is alliteration in this line through the repetition of the letter 'o' at the beginning of closely connected words.
17	B	Text (lines 16-17): 'Clara ... their trophy winning horse...'. A metaphor is used in this phrase. A metaphor is when two things are compared by saying something is something else. In this phrase, Clara is the 'trophy winning horse.'
18	A	Text (line 31): '...she found a gentleman of suitable wealth and esteem.' Esteem means have respect and admiration.
19	C	Text (lines 30-31): The underlined word is an adjective as it is describing the noun reputation.

ENGLISH: TEST A

Question	Answer	Explanation
20	A	The word potent means powerful and its antonym is inadequate which means lacking.
21	B	The word 'meticulous' means showing a great attention to detail; very careful and diligent.
22	B	All these words are verbs. Verbs are action or being words.
23	C	The word winsome means charming and sweet—endearing.
24	B	The words always and subtly are adverbs as they both describe verbs.
25	D	Entire Text: As this story reveals the motives for the Evil Stepmother's actions, her love for her two daughters, it makes the reader question whether Ana Tremaine is actually a villain.
26	B	The incorrectly spelt word is 'there' - the correct spelling is 'their'.
27	D	The incorrectly spelt word is 'lye' - the correct spelling is 'lie'.
28	N	There are no spelling mistakes on this line.
29	A	The incorrectly spelt word is 'buisness' - the correct spelling is 'business'.
30	B	The incorrectly spelt word is 'hankerchief' - the correct spelling is 'handkerchief'.
31	A	The incorrectly spelt word is 'carefuly' - the correct spelling is 'carefully'.
32	A	The incorrectly spelt word is 'goverment' - the correct spelling is 'government'.
33	A	The incorrectly spelt word is 'decideing' - the correct spelling is 'deciding'.
34	A	There should be a capital letter for 'folklore' as it is the start of a sentence.
35	D	There should be no apostrophe for 'Brother's' as there is no possession or omission.
36	A	There should be a capital letter for 'german' as it is a name of a language/nationality.
37	N	There are no mistakes in this line.
38	D	There should be a start of a new sentence after 'people' with the correct punctuation used.
39	D	The word Grimms should have an apostrophe Grimms' to show possession by two people (The Brothers Grimm).
40	N	There are no mistakes in this line.
41	B	There should be no colon as the words 'such as' already communicate the start of a list.
42	D	The correct preposition here is 'upon'.
43	B	The only option that is an adjective and fits into the context here is 'helpless'.
44	C	The correct pronoun here is 'whom'.
45	A	The correct conjunction here is 'although'.
46	C	The only option that is a noun and fits into the context here is 'kindness'.
47	E	The correct pronoun here is 'their'.
48	A	The correct conjunction here is 'When'.
49	B	The correct future tense here is 'take'.
50	C	The correct noun here is 'life'.

ENGLISH: TEST B

Question	Answer	Explanation
1	B	Text (lines 1-3): 'The storm cleared up below, for Mrs. March came home, and, having heard the story, soon brought Amy to a sense of the wrong she had done her sister.'
2	A	The phrase is a metaphor as Jo's book is being directly compared to a sprout.
3	D	Jo was not angry with the Amy for the destruction of her book because she had put half a dozen fairy tales into the book. The other options are reasons as to why Jo is angry over the destruction of her book.
4	C	Text (lines 26-28): '...the wisest course was to wait till some little accident, or her own generous nature, softened Jo's resentment and healed the breach.'
5	D	Text (lines 28-32): 'It was not a happy evening... something was wanting, and the sweet home peace was disturbed.' The 'something' that they want is peace.
6	B	This phrase is a simile as it compares two things using the word 'as'.
7	A	Text (lines 39-41): '...don't let the sun go down upon your anger. Forgive each other, help each other, and begin again tomorrow.' Jo's mother is asking Jo to forgive Amy before she goes to sleep.
8	C	Text (lines 46-48): 'Jo...said gruffly because Amy was listening, "It was an abominable thing, and she doesn't deserve to be forgiven."' Jo wants Amy to know she has not forgiven her.
9	E	Lines 51-63 mentions all of the options for how Amy responds to Jo for not forgiving her.
10	C	Text (line 65): 'He is always kind and jolly'. Also, in lines 84-86, Laurie tests the ice before they race upon it. This evidence shows that Laurie is sensible and friendly.
11	B	Text (lines 67-70): 'Amy... looked out with an impatient exclamation. "There! She promised I should go next time, for this is the last ice we shall have."'
12	A	The whole text: Amy loses her temper quickly, does not want to wait for Jo to forgive her and thinks very highly of her own virtues.
13	D	Text (lines 84-88): Laurie is checking to see if the warm spell that preceded the cold snap has made the ice thinner and thus unsafe to travel on before they start their race.
14	C	The phrase contains personification as an non-human thing, anger, has been given human qualities.
15	D	We know that Jo is feeling angry towards Amy after their fight. This phrase is a metaphor, so it cannot be taken literally. It is actually comparing Jo's anger to being a demon which is telling her to do a bad thing.
16	E	Text (110-117): Jo does try to 'rush forward' to help Amy but 'her feet seemed to have no strength in them'. We know this often happens when we are terrified. Thus, Jo is in fear for Amy's life and this fear is keeping her motionless.
17	D	Text (lines 121-134): To rescue Amy they used a rail from the fence, walked her home as fast as they could and Laurie put his coat around her to keep her warm.
18	B	Text (lines 141-143): 'Jo, looking remorsefully at the golden head, which might have been swept away from her sight forever under the treacherous ice.'
19	B	Text (lines 11-13): 'It seemed a small loss to others, but to Jo it was a dreadful calamity...' From the context, we know that this loss must be an awful disaster. The word catastrophe means disaster.
20	C	Text (51-55): 'Amy was much offended that her overtures of peace had been repulsed, and began ... to plume herself on her superior virtue.' In this context, Amy is praising herself for trying to make peace with Jo. The word commend means praise.

ENGLISH: TEST B

Question	Answer	Explanation
21	C	Text (lines 53-55): '...to plume herself on her superior virtue in a way that was particularly exasperating.' This question relies on your inference skills. If somebody is praising themselves for their own virtues, they would become quite irritating to listen to. Exasperating means irritating. The antonym of exasperating is delightful.
22	A	All these words are adverbs as they all describe verbs or adjectives.
23	D	Pride is the abstract noun as it is a name given to a concept that we cannot touch or feel.
24	E	Text (60-63): 'Amy kept making remarks about people who were always talking about being good and yet wouldn't even try when other people set them a virtuous example.' In this context, a virtuous example must be an example of someone being good. The word virtuous means ethical.
25	B	The passage is based on a family who live in the real-life world in historical America, but the family created is fictional. The genre is real-life fiction.
26	D	The incorrectly spelt word is 'posessed' - the correct spelling is 'possessed'.
27	B	The incorrectly spelt word is 'judgemant' - the correct spelling is 'judgement'.
28	D	The incorrectly spelt word is 'excelent' - the correct spelling is 'excellent'.
29	D	The incorrectly spelt word is 'new' - the correct spelling is 'knew'.
30	B	The incorrectly spelt word is 'knowlege' - the correct spelling is 'knowledge'.
31	B	The incorrectly spelt word is 'abilitys' - the correct spelling is 'abilities'.
32	C	The incorrectly spelt word is 'sorows' - the correct spelling is 'sorrows'.
33	B	The incorrectly spelt word is 'generus' - the correct spelling is 'generous'.
34	B	There should be a question mark before the closing speech marks.
35	B	The apostrophe should be after the 'r' for the word 'sisters' to show singular possession.
36	B	There should be a full stop after 'hand' as it is the end of the sentence.
37	A	There should be a comma before the start of the speech.
38	A	There should be a comma before the start of the speech and not a dash.
39	A	There should be a comma before 'not' as there is an embedded clause.
40	D	There should be a comma after 'leave' as a comma should come after the dependent clause when a dependent clause begins a sentence.
41	B	There should be an apostrophe after the t in 'Lets' to show omission.
42	C	The only option which agrees with the plural and the context is 'goddesses'.
43	B	The correct connective here is 'also'.
44	D	The only option which agrees with the context and is the correct noun is 'cycle'.
45	C	The correct word for the context that is possessive is 'heaven's'.
46	B	The only option which is a preposition and agrees with the context here is 'through'.
47	B	The correct conjunction here is 'after'.
48	E	The correct present tense verb here is 'is'.
49	A	The correct conjunction here is 'Moreover'.
50	B	The correct conjunction here is 'which'.

ENGLISH: TEST C

Question	Answer	Explanation
1	B	Whole text: The 'Preface' is the title given to the first part of the text, before the letters, which explains who the letters are written by and what subjects they discuss.
2	D	Text (10-16): '…if the reader.. has not the discernment to distinguish that natural elegance…let him lay the book down…' Astell is saying that if the reader cannot see the ex-cellence of the letters, he should stop reading the book.
3	C	Text (lines 11-14): Astell praises the 'delicacy of … observation' in Montague's writing. In this context, delicacy means exquisiteness. Frailty means weakness.
4	E	Text (lines 19-20): '…when I had it in my hands, how was it possible to part with it?' The rhetorical question is being used to emphasise how good Astell found the letters be and thus to also encourage the reader to read it as well.
5	D	Text (lines 22-25): '…the most ingenious author has condemned it to obscurity during her life; and conviction, as well as deference, obliges me to yield to her reasons.'
6	E	Text (lines 32-35): '…whilst it is surfeited with Male travels, all in the same tone, and stuffed with the same trifles; a lady has the skill to strike out a new path, and to embellish a worn-out subject with a variety of fresh and elegant entertainment.'
7	A	Text (lines 33-46): B to E are all mentioned as reasons why Lady Montague's account is better than a man's. However, Astell says that the purity of style comes from the standard of the English language 'besides the purity of style (for which it may justly, be accounted the standard of the English tongue)', which is used by both men and women.
8	D	Text (lines 47-52): '…let her own gender at least, do her justice; lay aside diabolical Envy…pleased that a woman triumphs'. Astell asks women to praise Montague's triumphs rather than to feel envious.
9	C	Text (lines 48-52): '…let her own gender at least, do her justice…let us freely own the superiority, of this sublime genius… pleased that a woman triumphs, and proud to follow in her train.' Astell is asking to reader to feel joy that a woman has triumphed and be inspired to triumph over men in their own subjects as well.
10	E	In the Preface, Astell praises Lady Montague's writing and states that all women should be pleased that Lady Montague, a woman, has written such great works.
11	A	Text (lines 58-68): Lady Montagu states that they had the 'ill fortune of a storm' and they were 'tossed very handsomely' and that she does not 'suffer from fear nor seasickness'. It does not mention the sailors guidance of the yacht or that she feared terrible storms.
12	D	Text (lines 79-81): Lady Montague writes 'the Dutch maids washing the pavement… with more application than ours do our bed-chambers.' Therefore, the Dutch maids clean their town with more dedication than the British ones.
13	C	Text (lines 83-85): 'Tis certain no town can be more advantageously situated for commerce. Here are seven large canals, on which merchant ships come up to the very doors of their houses.'
14	D	Text (lines 97-107): 'It will go a great way in making me satisfied with it, if it affords me an opportunity of entertaining you…I expect returns of all the London news. You see I have already learnt to make a good bargain…'
15	B	In the text Lady Montague comments 'I rather fancy myself upon parties of pleasure, than upon the road…'(Lines 114-115). This is something that Lady Montague imagines she is doing and not something that she is actually doing on her journey to make it pleasant.
16	B	Text (lines 136-137): 'Upon my word, I can yet find none, that is not dearer than you may buy it at London.' In this context, dearer means nicer.
17	C	Text (lines 57 & 110) 'Rotterdam, Aug. 3. O. S. 1716. ' & 'Hague, Aug. 5. O. S. 1716.'

Question	Answer	Explanation
18	E	Lady Montague is adventurous and spirited as she is going on an adventurous tour around several countries which she is very happy about. She is shown to be generous as she is looking for some lace for one of her friends.
19	B	Obscurity means the state of being unknown which is a synonym for anonymity.
20	E	Text (line 35): 'the vivacity and spirit which enliven every part'. Vivacity is a synonym of spirit. The antonym of vivacity is indifference which means a lack of concern.
21	C	Personification is when a human characteristic is given to something non-human. In this line non-human things, feelings, have been given human emotions and a human connection.
22	C	All these words are types of nouns (the names of people, places or things).
23	D	Text (line 65): 'were all Sunday night tossed very handsomely.' In this context, handsomely is means thoroughly and describes the way the passengers were tossed.
24	B	Text (line 97): 'You see, hitherto, I make no complaints'. Hitherto means until now. It is an adverb (it describes a verb or adjective). It is telling the reader when the verb occurred.
25	B	Non-Fiction is prose writing that is informative or factual rather than fictional.
26	B	The incorrectly spelt word is 'creater' - the correct spelling is 'creator'.
27	D	The incorrectly spelt word is 'maner' - the correct spelling is 'manner'.
28	A	The incorrectly spelt word is 'impresion' - the correct spelling is 'impression'.
29	A	The incorrectly spelt word is 'autobiograpy' - the correct spelling is 'autobiography'.
30	B	The incorrectly spelt word is 'falt' - the correct spelling is 'fault'.
31	N	There are no mistakes in this line.
32	D	The incorrectly spelt word is 'ummoral' - the correct spelling is 'immoral'.
33	D	The incorrectly spelt word is 'expres' - the correct spelling is 'express'.
34	C	There should be a comma between the coordinating adjectives 'crashing, roaring'.
35	B	There should be an apostrophe before the s in the word its as there is an omission— it's.
36	A	There should be an apostrophe in the word necklaces as the jewels belong to the necklace— necklace's.
37	D	There should be a comma after 'grey' as the phrase is an embedded clause.
38	C	There should be no comma after 'hair' as a comma cannot join two main clauses.
39	A	There should be an apostrophe in the word couldn't as there is an omission—couldn't.
40	D	There should be a question mark as the sentence is a question.
41	D	The name 'dali' should have a capital letter as it is a proper noun.
42	A	The only option that is singular and is in present tense here is 'smudge'.
43	B	The correct verb that fits the context here is 'look'.
44	E	The correct preposition here is 'with'.
45	D	The correct present perfect tense here is 'have been'.
46	A	The correct preposition here is 'over'.
47	C	The correct auxiliary verb that fits into the context here is 'must'.
48	D	The only option which is an adverb and fits the context here is 'carefully'.
49	B	The correct determiner here is 'My'
50	E	The correct verb in the present tense that fits the context here is 'shout'.

ENGLISH: TEST D

Question	Answer	Explanation
1	C	The rhyme scheme is ABCB as the words at the end of lines 2 and 3 rhyme.
2	C	Text (lines 6-8): 'The sweet buds every one, / When rocked to rest on their mother's breast,/ As she dances about the sun.' It is not the cloud that dances beneath the sun.
3	A	Text (line 14): 'And their great pines groan aghast...'. Aghast means appalled.
4	E	The thunder is described as struggling and howling against being fettered, whereas the lightning is guiding the cloud with a gentle movement. Therefore, the lightning is both more tender and more powerful than the thunder.
5	B	Text (line 18): 'Lightning my pilot sits'. A pilot controls the flight of an aircraft.
6	D	Text (21-26): 'Over earth and ocean...Over the rills, and the crags, and the hills,/Over the lakes and the plains'. The repetition of the word 'over' draws the reader's attention to the many places that the Cloud travels across.
7	D	Text (line 29): 'I all the while bask in Heaven's blue smile'. Bask means to delight in and 'Heaven's blue smile' refers to a nice blue sky. Benevolence means kindness.
8	E	Assonance is the repetition of vowel sounds in a line of text. In this line, the vowel 'a' is repeated.
9	D	Text (line 34): 'When the morning star shines dead'. The morning star is the sun and the sun shining dead refers to how even though the sun has set, the light from the sun can still be seen.
10	C	Aëry means light. Intangible means untouchable. The Cloud is at rest and so feels peaceful.
11	E	Stanza two, with the thunder howling against constraints and the lightning being lured by love, has a more passionate mood than stanza three.
12	A	Text (lines 45-46): 'That orbèd maiden with white fire laden, / Whom mortals call the Moon'.
13	C	Glide means to move smoothly and gently. The alliteration in the phrase draws the reader's attention to this movement over the Cloud.
14	B	Text (lines 49-51): 'And wherever the beat of her unseen feet, / Which only the angels hear, / May have broken the woof of my tent's thin roof'. The Moon's 'unseen feet' break through the roof and so it is describing the Moon's rays of light breaking through the hole in the tent.
15	D	Text (lines 70-72): 'Is the million-coloured bow; / The sphere-fire above its soft colours wove, / While the moist Earth was laughing below.' The text is describing a rainbow being created. There is nothing to say that the laughter is mocking, so the laughter is joyful.
16	B	Text (line 74): 'And the nursling of the Sky'. A nursling is a baby.
17	C	Whimsical means playful and mischievous, inconstant means frequently changing and influential means to have great influence over someone or something else. All of which apply to the Cloud.
18	E	The Cloud is described as having the power to create many things that influence our lives, such as rain, lightning and thunder. The poem describes how joy is discovered through these creations— nature is described as laughing and dancing throughout the passage.
19	D	Text (lines 19-20): 'In a cavern under is fettered the thunder, / It struggles and howls at fits'. The thunder is struggling against something, so it has been constrained.
20	C	Text (lines 31-32): 'The sanguine Sunrise, with his meteor eyes'/ And his burning plumes outspread'. The description of the Sunrise is passionate and positive. Therefore, the antonym to sanguine must be a negative word which fits into the context. Melancholy means sad which is an antonym of sanguine. Sanguine means cheerful.

Question	Answer	Explanation
21	E	Text (lines 55-57): 'When I widen the rent in my wind-built tent, / Till calm the rivers, lakes, and seas, / Like strips of the sky fallen through me on high'. In this context, the 'rent' is a tear in the in the tent. Rupture means tear.
22	C	Verbs are action or being words. All the words apart from 'through' are action words. 'Through' is an adverb. An adverb is a word which describes a verb or adjective.
23	D	All the words are adjectives. Adjectives are words that describe nouns.
24	B	An adverb is a word which describes a verb or adjective. The word 'never' describes the adjective 'stain', which is describing the 'pavilion of Heaven'.
25	D	Personification is when a non-human thing is given human characteristics. The entire poem uses personification as the Cloud is the narrator discussing its feelings and actions.
26	C	The incorrectly spelt word is 'siting' - the correct spelling is 'sitting'.
27	A	The incorrectly spelt word is 'hole' - the correct spelling is 'whole'.
28	C	The incorrectly spelt word is 'voluntered' - the correct spelling is 'volunteered'.
29	C	The incorrectly spelt word is 'pleasent' - the correct spelling is 'pleasant'.
30	C	The incorrectly spelt word is 'lonly' - the correct spelling is 'lonely'.
31	N	There are no mistakes in this line.
32	D	The incorrectly spelt word is 'pased' - the correct spelling is 'passed'.
33	C	The incorrectly spelt word is 'aproaching' - the correct spelling is 'approaching'.
34	N	There are no mistakes in this line.
35	A	There should be a closing bracket after 'dusk'.
36	D	There should be a full stop after 'bill' and a capital letter for 'these' as a new sentence has started.
37	D	There should not be a comma after 'need' as there should not be an embedded clause.
38	N	There are no mistakes in this line.
39	A	There are should be no full stop after 'large' as the sentence has not ended.
40	C	There should be a comma after 'Moreover' as the following phrase is an embedded clause.
41	C	There should be no colon after 'to' as neither a list nor an explanation has been given.
42	D	A pronoun must be used and the correct pronoun here is 'which'.
43	B	The correct conjunction here is 'however'.
44	A	The correct connective here is 'because'.
45	D	The correct adjective which fits into the context of the sentence is 'hot'.
46	C	The only option that agrees with the plural that must be used is 'several'.
47	C	The correct conjunction here is 'Despite'.
48	B	The only option in the correct future tense is 'will be'.
49	B	The correct past participle here is 'gotten'.
50	A	The only option that fits into the context of the sentence and is a superlative adjective is 'strongest'.

Other Titles in the First Past The Post® Series

English: Comprehensions

All books in this series contain 10 tests, each comprising a long passage with 15 accompanying questions. These tests are designed to be representative of the standard comprehension section of contemporary multi-discipline 11 plus and Common Entrance exams. Questions test the student's ability to extract factual information or draw inferences from the text, and some test the student's knowledge of vocabulary, grammar or literary techniques. All questions are multiple-choice, and full answers and explanations are included. Each book allows access to our Peer-Compare Online system, which assesses the candidate's performance anonymously on a question-by-question basis.

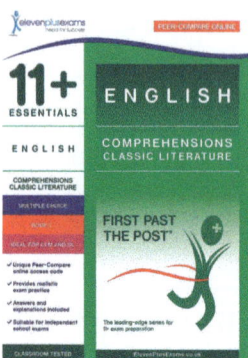

Classic Literature

All 10 passages in these books are taken from classic fiction books, such as those by Charles Dickens and Louisa May Alcott. These passages contain more challenging vocabulary than modern literature.

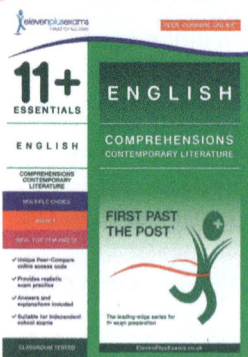

Contemporary Literature

All 10 passages in these books are written in the style of modern fiction books, using contemporary vocabulary.

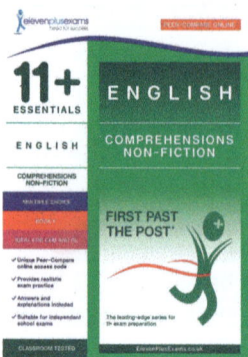

Non-Fiction

All 10 passages in these books are modern non-fiction pieces, such as opinion pieces, reviews and journal articles.